AMAZING CARDS

Fortune Telling with Playing Cards

This book is much easier to master than reading the more esoteric tarot cards.

Whether you want to gain a basic understanding of card reading, or you wish to master the cards and give readings for extra cash, *Amazing Cards : Fortune Telling with Playing Cards* is the perfect book for you. Best of all, if you have a playing deck at home, you can begin telling fortunes within minutes to gain insight into the future and hidden influences at work in your life right now!

AMAZING CARDS

Fortune Telling With Playing Cards

SOPHIA

New Age Books

ISBN: 81-7822-093-8

First Indian Edition: 2003

Fourth Printing: USA, 1999
(Published under the title "Furtune Telling with Playing Cards"
by Llewellyn Publications, USA)

Published by
NEW AGE BOOKS
A-44 Naraina Phase-I
New Delhi-110 028 (INDIA)
Email: nab@vsnl.in
Website: www.newagebooksindia.com

For Sale in Southeast Asia Only

Printed in India
at Shri Jainendra Press
A-45 Naraina Phase-I, New Delhi-110 028

Dedication

This book is lovingly dedicated to my grandparents, Vivian and Eva Luce.

Special thanks to Denny
for all his love and support
and thank-you Stella.

PUBLISHERS NOTE

NEW AGE BOOKS does not participate in, endorse, or have any authority or responsibility concerning private business transactions between our authors and the public. All mail addressed to the author is forwarded but the publisher cannot, unless specifically instructed by the author, give out an address or phone number.

CONTENTS

Illustrations

INTRODUCTION

The Cards and I

My grandmother passed down the practice of reading cards to me just as it had been passed down to her—from mother to daughter and grandmother to granddaughter for generations in my family. When my grandmother began to teach me how to read the cards, I was only three years old. She told me that no part of the technique was to be written down. Her reasons were that I was too young to read and that writing down instructions would somehow diminish the power of the cards. She stressed the importance of memorizing the cards and learning their subtleties by using them daily.

Early Instruction

At the end of the school day, most children arrive home to a snack and then start their homework. They read their textbooks and memorize their multiplication tables. I did not. Every day after school, my grandmother sat me down and we practiced my divination.

First, she separated all the cards into their suits and flipped them numerically from two up to the ace, repeating the meaning of each card until I memorized it. She taught me that although the way a person interprets the cards is different, the art relied on memorization. The important thing, she said, was to get a feel for the cards and know the hidden meaning behind each one. Throughout each afternoon, we went slowly over each card to absorb its meaning.

Every morning, we pulled one card to see what kind of day we would have. If the card did not make much sense, we pulled another card and laid it horizontally over the first one, forming a cross (literally meaning that the second card crosses you or gives you clear insight into what is really going on). Working mornings and afternoons with the cards proved to be a wonderful way to understand how each card worked with the others. Constant study of the cards cleared up any confusion.

Part of my teaching included working with face cards. My grandmother would ask me to pull out all the face cards and guess the person in my life each card represented. Studying the cards and matching them to people I knew was a wonderful way to practice the cards. We spent hours pinpointing which card represented which person (the queen of clubs was my grandmother). If I could not pinpoint a person in one of the cards that showed up, my grandmother had me put the card on my altar. She said that the person would come to me—and he or she always did.

I began to concentrate on mastering the Small Star spread—a simple, four-card layout, which is great for beginners. I did that layout every day until I got the hang of it. With my grandmother's help, I soon had the meaning of each card completely understood.

My daily study of the deck and practice of layouts—and my grandmother's personal hints and ideas—helped me to completely understand the cards. I saw how they related to one another and how, when they touch each other, one card interacts with the others surrounding it in a very magical but very real way. What does it mean to have two cards touch each other? The possibilities seemed endless for me.

For more practice, I read for my friends and family. I also read to strangers who had come to our house to have their futures told. I began to find that reading the cards was easier with strangers because you can just go ahead and read them—family and friends ask too many questions. My grandparents were impressed that I was good at reading cards and continued to encourage me. I started to have my own clientele—some clients I see even today.

I soon graduated and began to read complex spreads, including the Wheel of Life, which is still my favorite because it includes my love of astrology.

Family

From the 1920s through the 1970s, my grandparents helped many people by reading the cards. Their readings provided hope and the ability to see problems clearly. My grandparents had made a name for themselves in their community and were known as reliable readers and were excellent at what they did. The playing cards were my grandmother's system and way of reading. My grandfather read coffee grounds and tea leaves, used palmistry, and did crystal ball readings. A steady stream of visitors needing advice visited our home. During this time, however, readers traditionally did not accept money or a fixed fee. Clients paid by donation or by bringing a present (usually food). Also at this time, readers did not set a fixed time for the readings—readings took as long or as short as was necessary, depending on the client.

As I grew up, my grandparents told me that I had a gift from God, and that I should never use it lightly. Although they did not want me to live a life of poverty, they knew that my destiny was to be a psychic. Because at that time psychics did not charge for their services, they were not sure how I would survive on my own.

It was my Great Aunt Loria, my grandfather's eldest sister, who set into motion events that led me to begin accepting money for psychic services. Loria had the family nickname of "Diamond Loria" and was one of the most famous psychics in our family. She was an outgoing, opinionated woman and, because she was the eldest sister, my grandfather listened to her and my grandmother admired her. She convinced my grandparents that I should be a writer (you see how psychic she was?) and that to record stories was very important. She told them I could reach many people with the gift, teach others to read cards for themselves, and also support myself. My grandparents agreed, and told me everything about psychic traditions that they knew so that I could record what was important.

My great aunt encouraged me to receive just fees for my services and to write of my experiences. When she visited me, she read and critiqued every story I had written about the psychic world. Then she would tell me another true story of the supernatural. We always had FATE magazine around our home, and my great aunt believed that someday I would write for that magazine in addition to writing books.

All of this teaching and learning took place over twenty years ago, and these people are "on the other side" now, but I remember all the lessons they taught me.

The Amazing Cards

It is truly amazing how accurate the cards are and how specific cards show up at the right places in a reading at the right times. I am fascinated that the cards can explain a certain circumstance better than anything else.

When I was in my twenties, an old Gypsy woman who practiced in a town near my home read the cards for me. This reading was a pivotal moment in my life—I was transformed by a complete stranger who knew so much about me. She knew my past and my present. She told me who I would marry and the life I would lead. So far, everything has come true. Her accuracy not only as a gifted psychic but also as a gifted reader changed my life. Before I went to her, I thought I would spend my life in my small town. It never occurred to me that what she predicted would transpire. Was it just her reading or did she give me the courage to dream and make my life better? After that reading, I gathered my nerve and challenged myself into creating a better reality. When that door popped open, I decided I wanted to do the same for others.

The best compliment I received about the cards was from a gentleman client who had never had a reading before. I was involved in a benefit to raise money to fight AIDS. The event was held in Tokyo in an old Buddhist temple that dated from the twelfth century. I was reading the cards for whoever sat down at my table. This man sat in front of me and said that since it was Halloween he was in the mood for a reading. As I told his fortune, he and his friend were astounded by the cards' accuracy. After the reading, he looked under the table and asked how I did it. I just laughed and told him that was the magic of the cards.

I believe one reason the cards work is that they are archetypes of our subconscious, and that they reveal certain hidden truths to us. Without the cards, it is harder to intercept the meaning of what our inner self is trying to tell us—the cards are an easy, accurate way to access what we need to know. We can use this information to make more sense of our lives or make some decision about the future. Card readings are a little insurance to help us through life.

The Formation of This Book

For many years, I did not think much about these past events. My life began to go in many different paths and I did not spend time being a writer until recently. I did, however, keep the grimores, the tools of the family trade, and the secrets with me, and I kept doing readings and getting better.

Twenty years later, Llewellyn Publications published my husband's book, *Global Ritualism*. To publicize the book, we attended the annual American Booksellers Association Convention. By this time, I was an established professional psychic reader and Llewellyn's staff asked me to do quick readings. Cartomancy readings are what I do when I have many readings to do. I found myself at this huge convention reading cards for an endless line of people. At the convention, I met Sandra Weschcke, who encouraged me to write a book about the playing cards. While I read the cards for her and her lovely family, they convinced me to begin writing. I was excited about the possibility—here was the fulfillment of my grandparent's and great aunts' dreams.

I decided to ask elders in my family what I should do. I turned to my mother and cousin, who was in her eighties. When I told her the proposal, my cousin just laughed and said, "You mean people are interested in this after all these years? Sure, why not!" My mother, who also knows how to read, urged me to go for it.

As I wrote this book, I searched for history about how playing cards became used for divination. I had information that was orally handed down in my family, but I wanted to know more about the history of card reading. One day I visited Stargazers, a store in Bellevue, Washington, where I sometimes do readings. Tess, the owner, approached me and said she wanted to return a book that I had left there. She handed me a book titled *Fortune Telling by Cards* by Professor P. R. S. Foli. The book was so old that no date of publication was on it. My mouth fell open. I told her that it was not my book. "Of course it is," Tess proclaimed. "You're writing a book on playing cards and I found it in my office with a note on it." The note read "Sophia" in a handwriting we did not recognize. I was shocked. I had never seen this book before, yet it was a missing bit of the cartomancy puzzle I had been seeking. The discovery of this book was wonderfully weird—I could now finish my own manuscript. Tess tracked down the book's owner who was gracious enough to lend it to me. We still do not know how the book came to her office or why it had my name on it. Some things cannot be explained, and I have to thank Professor Foli for the ingenious way he sent me the book from beyond.

Because the art of reading cards is an oral tradition, it has almost been forgotten today. I have met few people who know how to use the cards, and the ones who do whom I have encountered have been taught by a family member. The main focus of this book is to supply information on a forgotten tradition and perhaps bring back the amazing interest in cartomancy that used to be so prevalent.

As you begin to use this book, realize that for some people card reading and fortune telling is very serious. Some may want to use this book only for entertainment—which is fine—but be clear on what you are doing. Is card reading "for real" or a game? It cannot be both at the same time. I use card reading for both at different times, and I encourage you to try it both ways, too. I suspect that your respect for the cards will grow as mine did and you will eventually take it more seriously than not.

You can use the cards in the spreads explained in this book. I have seen other ways of laying out the cards, but, in my opinion, they are not as accurate as the ones you will find in this book. It is easier, before you hang out your shingle as a playing card reader, to practice on everyone until you get the hang of the spreads. Reading astrology books or books on numerology will help you gain insight. An amazing number of Tarot readers enjoy cartomancy because it is fun to learn another way to read, and many are already good at reading cards and can enhance themselves as a reader. The great benefit of the cards over the Tarot is that the cards are more down-to-earth and practical, they are less mystical and therefore more direct! Enjoy, learn and prosper!

Preparing Yourself

How do you get started reading cards? It could not be easier. All you need is a deck of regular playing cards. Use this deck only for reading the cards. I have created a special deck of cards (the Sophia deck) to read with. They are made specifically for card readings and you will not find anything else on the market that lends itself to cartomancy in such a way.

The best time for a reading is whenever you feel the urge. You will need a quiet room and a table that provides at least two feet of space between you and the person you are giving a reading to. The person you are doing a reading for should always sit across from you. Cards and card readings have been traditionally passed down in families, especially between women. In my family it went like this: from Grandmother, to mother, to daughter. Most of us always do our readings either in the kitchen or near it. I always tape my readings and give my clients the only copy of the tape.

Recently we converted a garden shed in our back garden to use as a place to do readings. We added more windows and refinished the inside with homey objects and furniture. To get to our garden shed you must wander through a formal flower garden.

I am not suggesting that you go through all this trouble to create such a special place to give readings, but whatever place you do choose, it should have a warm, inviting atmosphere. Just a couple of candles and a table will do the trick.

Before you begin reading the cards with a regular deck, remove the jokers and shuffle the cards many times, thinking about what kind of reader you want to be and your purpose for learning about the cards. By focusing on the cards as you shuffle, you will gain insight and direction. The main part of connecting with the cards is to get comfortable with them, which is easy to do because they are universal and familiar. Some people initiate their cards by lighting a white candle for clarity and throwing salt around the cards. I suggest this ritual if you want to protect yourself.

Sleep with the cards and carry them about; make them yours. Once you start reading the cards, keep trying until you have a strong feeling about them. Some may try reading the cards a few times and put them down for later; others will become professional readers. You must decide what kind of reader you will become. Much of that decision depends on your relationship with the cards.

If you are going to give readings to others, that is great; but do not suffer with people who are disrespectful. It is not up to you to convince rude people that you are a reader. Stay away from people who have been drinking or taking drugs or medications; they are nearly impossible to read, so do not waste your time.

I hope that this book will help you find another way to look at the world and a way to develop your psychic ability. My grandparents wanted me to pass down the family tradition of fortune telling. This book is a promise kept to them.

CHAPTER 1

A Short History of the Cards

The history of playing cards goes back at least 500 years, though many people think playing cards were created over 1,000 years ago. The use of playing cards was first recorded in India and China. These early cards resembled the decks of today. People thought of the cards as accurate ways to predict the future and highly regarded any psychic or medium who had knowledge of them. It is widely believed that the cards came to Europe through the Gypsies. The tradition of playing cards traveled from Western Asia to Egypt, then to North Africa. From there, they finally surfaced in Europe.

One theory, however, states that the Arabs and Moors introduced the cards to the Spaniards in 1379. In Spain, people called the cards Naibi, which means "to foretell." Even according to this theory, though, the cards were first known for divination and not for playing games.

Regardless of where the cards originated, it was the Gypsies who preserved the art of cartomancy, and it was the Europeans who began to use the cards for amusement or to win money.

The earliest cards were Tarot cards. In the middle of the fourteenth century, people added numerical sequences to the four suits of the symbolic cards and used the cards to play games. By the fifteenth century, a deck was composed of seventy eight cards—twenty two symbolic cards and four suits divided into fifty six lesser cards. The lesser cards contained four court cards (King, Queen, Chevalier, and Valet) and ten point cards. The symbolic cards and one of the face cards was rejected, bringing the basic card deck to its present number of fifty two. The Spanish threw out the Queen; the French brought it back and tossed the Chevalier. The early German packs rejected the Queen and introduced the Obermann, a superior knight. The English had no preference and accepted either the French or Spanish decks.

Throughout all these additions and deletions, there have always been four suits—although not always similar to the present-day suits. The original four were: Cups (equaling faith), Swords (equaling justice), Coins (equaling money and charity), and Clubs (equaling strength). These suits still remain in old Spanish and Italian decks. Old German decks have four suits: Bells, Leaves, Hearts, and Acorns. During the fifteenth century, the French began using Spades, Hearts, Clubs, and Diamonds.

No one is sure why the present-day suits match the French style. My personal theory is because of the importance of the Queen. It is also important to note that the famous Mademoiselle Lenormand, who was Napoleon's cartomancy reader and who helped make cartomancy respectable, was French.

From the fifteenth century on, the hidden lore of the cards quietly spread throughout Europe and North and South America. Wherever gambling went, readings followed. In the early 1900s, several companies published the secret lore of the cards which spread knowledge of readings to many people. Interest peaked and then died away in the 1920s, and the tradition began to be handed down through family members and friends—just as Gypsies had been passing the knowledge to their family members all along.

CHAPTER 2

The Meanings of the Cards

Before you learn how to read the cards using different spreads—and before you begin doing card spells—you must have an idea of each card's meaning. As my grandmother taught me, the key to a good reading is memorizing the meaning of each card. This chapter lists the meaning of each suit and each card (including face cards, which always represent key people).

Use these meanings for all the spreads found in this book except the Wheel of Life spread. For that spread, use the meanings found in chapter 5, "Card Meanings for the Wheel of Life Spread."

♥ Hearts

The Hearts—well, nothing could be more romantic! Hearts is a suit full of love and romance, giving and receiving. This suit conjures up the images we get when love first starts to bloom. Wherever you find this suit, you know that love is just around the corner and that it is here to stay. Hearts are the source and key of all emotions and feelings. They are the center of love in the reading and mean that you are somehow near ultimate love. They do not necessarily mean a romantic love, however. Hearts can represent friendship, children, parents, or, for some, self-love. When looking at this suit, pose a question such as "For the long term, what do I want for myself?" Ask yourself how you feel about this current situation.

Hearts allow you to literally get to the heart of a matter. They indicate what you desire in life, your support people, and your feelings about certain ideas.

In the past, hearts only meant marriage, but today this idea has changed. Life is much more complicated now. With the introduction of mass transportation, television, telephones, and computers, our world has become much bigger. It is no longer possible to look at the cards and say you will be married soon. People today have more interesting lives and more control of their destiny than in past generations. When hearts come into a reading—no matter what layout or where they land—it is almost always a sign of good fortune. Hearts are images that indicate you can attract what you need and get what you want from others.

Ace of Hearts: An Overpowering Love.

The ace of hearts in any layout is a strong, intense card. In a reading, this card symbolizes that something great will happen to you. Any romantic encounter could be for life or for a change that will open up doors for you in a wild and loving way. This is a great card to use in a card spell attracting love, luck, and lust (see chapter 9). It is extremely passionate. Anywhere that this card falls indicates a strong-willed individual with gusto and spirit. If you have been lonely for a long time, you may meet someone who will change that.

In one reading, a woman received this card in the first house. She revealed that it was difficult to find someone who was attracted to her. All of her male friends treated her like one of the boys. I told her that with the ace of hearts here, this would change. It did; and she soon became romantically involved with one of her friends. The relationship surprised them both.

Two of Hearts: A Sweet Encounter.

The two of hearts is a minor card. It is the beginning card for relationships and is found in the starting of a relationship. Usually the card means flirtation or a pleasant encounter. It symbolizes warmth and coziness and is an excellent card for starting anything new involving warm feelings. It is not a powerful card unless it is used in a circle or spell; then it means that the home and the influences in that house are safe from harm.

Three of Hearts: Influencing Others.

The three of hearts is also a minor card, but it is stronger than the two of hearts. Relationships and particular friendships are what this card symbolizes, and it is the key point. When casting a spell using this card, remember that it is a friendship card and can influence friends, although not your best friends. The card is more for people outside your immediate circle—people you do not spend a lot of time with.

Four of Hearts: Realistic Love.

When this card appears, you are getting a realistic view on how your loved one really appears. It is the beginning of seeing the flaws in a relationship. Do not be overly critical of others, however, or you will end up sounding ungrateful (unless there is a concrete reason for your feelings).

Five of Hearts: Great Fortune.

The five of hearts is a very lucky card. It is the luckiest of all the heart cards and denotes the same benefits as the planet Jupiter (good luck, travel, higher knowledge, friendship, money, and health). It is a generous card and anywhere it is found you know you are surrounded by good fortune.

I call the five of hearts the insurance card and use it for many card spells, especially ones for protection.

Six of Hearts: Long-term Good Luck.

The six of hearts is a little stronger than the five. While the five of hearts is good luck, the six is more good luck that has been around for a while—only you may not have been using it to your benefit. This card is telling you to take notice of what is going on—and if you really have your heart set on something, you should go for it. This is a great card for going that extra mile for something you really want.

Seven of Hearts: Reunites People from the Past.
The seven of hearts is a romantic card, but it always concerns someone you have known for some time (sometimes an old flame). It could be an individual whom you never could get together with and now the cards are in your favor. It is a beautiful card that reunites old loves.

In one reading, the seven of hearts came up for a lonely widow who said, "I cannot possibly imagine who that could be." Then an old friend who had not seen her for twenty-five years called her out of the blue. They picked up where they left off so long ago; it was sweet to witness.

Eight of Hearts: An Intense Relationship.
The eight of hearts means a strong relationship, a close marriage, or business partners who share more than money. In a reading, friends who have a deep love for you can also show up as this card. It also is a card that means you are in a long-term relationship where everything is smooth. Use the eight of hearts in card spells for adding more depth to an established relationship.

This card came up in a reading where one friend was inquiring about another friend. The person was nursing the friend back to health. They had a beautiful platonic relationship.

Nine of Hearts: An Intelligent Fling.

The nine of hearts is a thinker's romantic card. It attracts people who fall in love with intelligent types. If you find that bookstores, libraries, and magazine stands are places where you enjoy spending time, you certainly could meet some literary types here. This is the "heart meets the mind" card.

One woman I know uses the nine of hearts in card spells when she wants to meet a new man. The men she meets are usually English teachers, and she always meets them in public libraries.

Ten of Hearts: Wonderful Rewards.

The ten of hearts is a combination of all the other cards before it. It is a card full of prosperity, romance, and love. It is not as strong as the ace of hearts, but this card would definitely be classified as second in strength. It also means it is the highest point of its kind and that things will be changing soon. If you receive this card in a reading, take advantage of the energy and use it to your benefit. This is a wonderful card for those with an impulsive nature. Use it in any of the houses for a winning love/good life card spell.

Face Cards

Jack of Hearts: A Light-haired, Young Individual. The jack of hearts represents a special type of person who may be entering your life. Sometimes it is someone you already know. Jack of hearts are usually young men with blond or dark blond hair, light eyes, and good physical bodies. They are sweet and strong, and they can also be shy. They like to please. They are good friends to have, but sometimes can be distant.

Occasionally a woman will be represented by a jack; these women are aggressive young go-getters and not shy at all. They will also be blond (they could be "bottled blonds") and have light-colored eyes.

Queen of Hearts: A Blond-haired, Blue-eyed Woman. The queen of hearts represents a mature woman who has blond hair, blue eyes, and a light complexion. Usually the queens are attractive people and the best-looking ones in the deck. Fun-loving and giving, the queen of hearts is a good person to know. She can be helpful. Look, however, at the cards around her. Those other cards will give more depth to her personality. Sometimes they reveal more sweetness and light, although that can be a mask for how they really feel. Many times they are the symbol for romance and love; a red rose and apple blossoms are this queen's symbols. Most of the time, it is a woman who is a close friend, but in many cases it is a lover. Sometimes it could be a man, but it would be someone who is very effeminate.

King of Hearts: A Blond-haired, Blue-eyed Man. The King of Hearts is the card of deep, long-lasting love. It represents an extended relationship with a mature blond or light-haired male. These men have blue eyes and a light complexion, and they are usually romantic and "true blue." They are well established in their beliefs and goals and have a clear vision. Look at the surrounding cards to make sure you understand the goals and desires of this king because so strong are their desires that they can run right over you. This is a passionate card.

The king of hearts could be a woman, but if it is, she is a very strong woman who runs her own company and takes care of everything herself, or she could be very masculine.

♣ Clubs

Work, work, work! Clubs signify working hard to achieve your goals. They are persistent and full of drive. They also can seem discouraging. It is hard to get what you want and everything seems like a fight in life, nothing is easy but sometimes everything comes your way. The clubs are the beginning of starting a new long-term project to reach a goal, such as going back to school, starting a new business from scratch or building a new home. Clubs rarely indicate small or short-term goals. Usually they indicate a long difficult process with frequently unrewarding goals until the end. These are the kind of works that never seem to finish, but when the work is finished you feel a profound sense of accomplishment. The clubs also provide insight into your blind or weak spots and clarity where there once was none. You can also find out what is going on with loved ones when you use these cards. The ace, of course, is the pinnacle of all these ideas.

Ace of Clubs: Major Transformation.

The ace of clubs is the most intense of all the clubs. It comes up in a reading where there is a major transformation about to take place. Usually this transformation is a goal you are pursuing. It shows up many times in a reading where a change of occupation takes place. The ace of clubs is about self-realization. It is a good card to use in a card spell to get yourself moving.

This card came up frequently for a client who used to visit me often. He had a hard time making up his mind about what he wanted to do. He had many talents, but was unsure which was the best path for him. Choosing a path was something he anguished over for a long time. I told him that not making a decision was a decision. He realized that he was holding himself back because of a lack of self-confidence and low self-esteem. After getting this card, he went into the music industry. Last time I heard from him, he was married with two kids and successful at his chosen profession.

Two of Clubs: Difficulties with Projects.

This card represents minor problems and difficulties either with starting something new or finishing old projects. This is the card of a procrastinator.

In one reading when this card came up, the client had a bad attitude so I asked about his problem. He said it was hard to get going on anything; he always found a reason not to do things and had a never-try attitude.

Three of Clubs: Major Responsibility.

The three of clubs is much responsibility, but not much reward. It is similar to having a life's work where the pay is low and the reward is nonexistent. When this card appears, it is not a good time for change. Everything leads to the understanding that this is a period of sticking things out.

Four of Clubs: Little Progress.

The four of clubs is clearly an indicator of those who are stuck in a rut. If you seem to be making little progress, it is the four of clubs at work. The positive response is that your vision is clearer and you are now in the process of completing what is next.

Five of Clubs: Small Accomplishments.

The five of clubs signifies that your hard work is starting to pay off, that you are starting to reap some of the benefits of all that you have accomplished—although you are far from done.

I have seen this card in readings when people think that they are further along then they really are. One example was a carpenter I saw who never finished his jobs properly and was always called back to do the job again.

Six of Clubs: Procrastination.
The six of clubs represents work you need to complete in a certain area in your life. Wherever this card falls, you will not be successful anywhere else until you complete what you need to do here. It is usually the kind of work you detest. The six of clubs shows where you tend to do the most procrastinating.

Seven of Clubs: Reflect on Your Plans.
The seven of clubs represents trial and error. It symbolizes that if at first you don't succeed, try, try again. Also, for some people who are in a period of reevaluating the wisdom of carrying on, this card may represent a goal that is not working out the way they planned. It is an important time to review and to reflect, and maybe try another strategy. If the first time did not work, think about what would make the second time more successful.

Eight of Clubs: Forge Ahead on All Plans.
The eight of clubs represents discouragement. It seems like you have worked so hard for so long and you have not gotten anywhere. Whatever project you are involved with, this is the wrong time to stop. Finish it—the eight of

clubs is testing you. It is similar to starting winter quarter classes and knowing that summer is a long way away.

Nine of Clubs: Work on Yourself.

The nine of clubs means that everything you have been trying to accomplish is almost done. You should be finishing up all projects and not starting anything new. This is a difficult card for those who never finish anything.

One man I read for who got this card said he loved to start new projects but hated to finish the ones he started. His partner said it was driving him crazy, but what could he do?

Ten of Clubs: Major Changes.

This is the last card of the numbered clubs and means that everything will soon change. You are at the top of the heap. How things change for you is up to you; this card represents the hard work you have done. If you have not paid attention and let details slip or were generally lazy, nothing much will happen. But if you worked hard and never lost sight of your dreams, then good fortune awaits you.

Face Cards

Jack of Clubs: A Brown-haired, Hazel-eyed Individual.

This card represents a person (either a female or male) with brown hair and light brown or hazel eyes who is usually a sturdy-looking individual. There is a special type of temperament to this person, usually strong-willed. He or she could be someone who is at odds with you because either you have a definite belief system the person disagrees with or the two of you cannot agree on many issues. Most people of this type earn a healthy respect from their peers.

Queen of Clubs: A Dark-haired, Hazel-eyed Woman.
The queen of clubs card represents a womanly type of person. Like the jack, this person has brown to dark-brown hair or black hair. This person has light-colored skin and hazel or light brown eyes; has much energy and drive; and pursues her own interest to perfection—this person knows what she wants out of life and how to get it. This is the type of person you want on your side for any business transaction; she gets what she wants out of life and is usually successful.

King of Clubs: A Dark-haired, Hazel-eyed Man.
The king of clubs usually represents a man. Men of this suit are level-headed and determined, they usually are serious and everything has a reason for them. The king of clubs has hair that is dark brown or a color that could be almost black at times. He might have some gray in his hair.

The king of clubs could be a woman, but this is a woman who is tough and aggressive and may be president of her own company. If a woman, she is equal to all her peers and has gotten where she is from working hard.

♦ Diamonds

Diamonds is a wonderful suit—it is the ultimate symbol of money, fun, excitement, pleasure, and insight. When everything is going great, you can believe that the energy of the diamonds is around. This suit represents things that happen with ease, including windfalls, surprise gifts, and new prosperity. If you want to get the ball rolling in your financial or personal life and you wish to achieve your dreams and desires, use this card in a spell. Watch it though—make sure you know what you want because this card could give you energy that is hard to control. It is similar to being on a roller-coaster ride—you might not know where you will end up, but the ride is incredible.

Diamonds can also be small gifts. In the lower numbers, they could represent things such as a discount at a favorite store or a loved one who gives you a gift. Not only are people with diamonds on the receiving end, but they are also on the giving side. Tight-fistedness is not the nature of the diamonds, nor have I seen the card show up for people who cannot share.

Diamonds are good cards to get, but remember that sometimes a gift can have some hidden meaning, especially if the cards around diamonds are not so positive.

One woman who used to see me unfortunately always got diamonds. Her cards around the diamonds told her to be cautious and that there would be a price to pay. The price was her freedom. She would please people, especially men, to get what she wanted. After a while, she wanted to know who she was and not just what she could get from people. It has taken her a while to get more perceptive in life.

The diamonds, like hearts, represent easiness in gaining desires—but are not all great. If it seems too good to be true, question it but take full advantage of what you want.

Ace of Diamonds: Money, Money, Money!

This is a fun card that represents a financial windfall for those who use it to their advantage. If you want something in your favor, the ace of diamonds will help you realize your dreams, no matter how far out they seem.

Two of Diamonds: A Turn Toward the Better.

The two of diamonds is present just when everything starts to go smoothly. Wherever this card ends up, life is pretty good and everything is looking up. Usually this card shows up wherever there has been a dry spell and you have just finished a difficult period in your life. When this card shows up, I tell my clients that everything will soon change. They always shrug and say, "It's about time."

Three of Diamonds: Desires Come True.

The three of diamonds reveals that life is how it should be. It is the yes card and means that what you desire almost always will come true if you really try.

One woman trying to buy a new car for the first time got this card in a reading. She finally got together the self-confidence to test drive the car she wanted. And yes, she did buy it.

Four of Diamonds: Taking Control.

The four of diamonds reveals that everything is going well and your life is taking a turn for the better—only you do not think everything is going your way. Sometimes you are suspicious of a gift and ask yourself, "What's the catch?"

I have seen this card in readings where the person in question had a difficult time trusting others.

Five of Diamonds: Go Out on a Limb.

The five of diamonds is a lucky card. Money, ideas, creativity, and relationships flow smoothly. Using this card in a card spell will help you gain quick success. Wherever this card hits, it indicates that all is on your side. Use this card to go after what really matters in your life. Do not waste your energy on small things—go for the big ticket items and take risks; remember, this is not a boring card.

Six of Diamonds: Creativity at an All-Time High.

The six of diamonds indicates that life is very intense right now. Whatever you do is happening at a rate ten times the norm. It is an intensely busy time and you must keep up with the demands others make on you. In short, it is a publish or perish time. This is a common card for creative people who—when they feel the urge to create—must do so at an accelerated pace.

Seven of Diamonds: A New Look.
If you ever wanted to completely change your looks and attitude, now is the time. The sky is the limit with the seven of diamonds. This change is much more intense then getting and putting on a decal—it is similar to getting a huge colorful tattoo or taking a leap into uncharted water. Do so with confidence and great verve.

One woman I saw was flat-chested and it really bothered her. She did what she had always wanted to and added a couple of inches. She was pleased by her new look.

Eight of Diamonds: Any Dream Is Possible.
Usually this card means yes—yes to any project, idea, goal, or dream; anything that you aspire to. In short, it is a green light in a big race that tells you to go.

In one reading, I had a married couple who wanted to know if they should buy a vacation home. Since it was a joint decision, I told them that this was the perfect time. They told me they had just started looking and had not decided where they wanted to buy. They either wanted the house to have a golf course nearby for him or be on a lake for her. They called me about two weeks after the reading to say they had found their dream home, with a lake in front of the house and a golf course behind it.

Nine of Diamonds: Expansion in Earthly Goods.
The nine of diamonds appears when you are near the completion of a project. Sometimes it can appear when everything has been going well for so long that you

expect it to continue. This card is saying that you should take another look at your circumstances and either forge ahead or take advantage of everything that is surrounding you.

Ten of Diamonds: Great Fortune, Great Luck.
The ten of diamonds is a lucky card indeed. It is a strong card for money, enjoyment, health, fun, and abundance. All the good things in life are exalted with this card. You can reach new heights and take full advantage of opportunities that are now surrounding you. When they get this card in a reading, I tell people that they must act immediately on whatever good is handed to them. If they do not take what is offered with a thank you, they will lose the offer of a lifetime.

Face Cards

Jack of Diamonds: Brown-haired, Green-eyed Person.
The jack of diamonds is a young go-getter who can be either male or female. If it is a woman, she is young, athletic, and usually has a clear idea what she wants and how she will get it. These people are dynamic, outgoing, and very motivated. Plenty of wonderful ideas surround these individuals—it is a shame if they are not taken seriously since they have so much to offer to others. Jack of diamonds have light to medium brown hair and pale to light brown skin. Occasionally they are redheaded. Their eyes can be hazel to green.

Queen of Diamonds: Brown-Haired, Green-Eyed. Woman. The queen of diamonds represents a woman with hair color ranging from light brown to chocolate-colored; they also can be red heads. They have either green or hazel eyes, although brown eyes are not uncommon. This card represents people who are fun, interesting, and may sometimes be shallow. They know how to make money and are resourceful. People genuinely like the people whom this card represents. Having a friend or lover like this can inspire jealousy in others; people wonder how you lucked out having a person like this in your life.

King of Diamonds: Brown-haired, Blue-eyed Man. The king of diamonds is a person with dark blond to brown hair or red hair. Usually this person has light-colored eyes, blue to hazel. Occasionally you will find a person with brown hair and brown eyes. This person usually has a sunny disposition, a talent for making money, and has an easy going style. The king of diamonds is a fortunate card—this person is not only a lot of fun but also genuine and can bring you good luck. This person can, however, be a bit intense at times.

♠ Spades

Spades represent the difficulties in life; the gray in clouds. The suit can range in degree from the times when nothing seems to go right to outright disasters. It is not a pleasant suit and you generally do not want it to show up in a reading you give yourself, but you can learn from it. I will not use spades in a card spell unless I want to stir up trouble for someone else—but that is a bad idea. So powerful are spades that, used negatively in a card spell against another, no amount of psychic protection will completely cover them from the unearthly backlash unleashed.

If a spade card shows up in a reading, it indicates a problem you have been having for a while. All of this can seem negative, but really it is not; spades can be wonderful too. They can show you insight where it might not have existed before. If you have a recurring problem, the spade will show you why that happens. It can show what you really need to work on to improve your world and how to have the courage to overcome obstacles. Spades, like tough things in life, are not for gutless people. The spades propel you into action to improve and repair what is really wrong. They will help people who want to improve their lot in life.

Ace of Spades: Death or Completion.

It is true that this card has a bad image and symbolizes death. It has, however, earned more of a bad reputation then it deserves. This bad reputation may have come about because of the dramatization of its meaning in the opera *Carmen.* When Carmen draws the ace of spades, she sings about her doomed fate.

Whatever the reason, though, remember that this card also means the end or the completion of something—either of a relationship you know of, your own relationship, a project, or whatever. All things have a beginning and the ace of spades is the completion of that cycle. The completion could be pleasant or unpleasant. It is a difficult card for those who are especially resistant to change. Sometimes this card will push someone into the next stage of development, especially for those who have been wishy-washy in the past. Whenever you see this card, remember that it takes much courage and inner wisdom to make the right choices. You must be strong in any decision you make at this time.

Two of Spades: Wistfulness.
The two of spades is a minor card. It comes up when there is a small problem (for example, you cannot find a parking space or your glasses) or a more serious one (perhaps you might be feeling that everything wonderful happens to others and life is passing you by). It is a wistful card.

Three of Spades: Superficiality or Stubbornness.
The three of spades is a harsh card. It indicates superficiality and the inability to make clear choices. Wherever this card lands, it says that what you need to look at

are serious issues. Even though this is not a wonderful card, it is a wake-up call to manage your own life and develop yourself.

I used to get this card a lot, especially as a teenager. In almost every reading I gave myself, this card appeared in my ninth house. This showed me that I was a person whose philosophy and higher knowledge were extremely lacking. Since it is such an unflattering card, I decided to change my way of looking at the world. I found a job teaching kids, read books, and had my first real boyfriend.

Four of Spades: Difficult Beginnings.

The four of spades is a card that indicates a very hard worker—someone who has tried for a long time to do something and has had little success. I have seen this card show up for people who are having an extremely hard time in a relationship and are about to quit. Although they have not made any changes, they are starting to look at other options.

This card appeared in a reading for a woman who was in an abusive relationship. She knew that she should move on, but was hoping her partner would change. She realized that he would not seek the help he desperately needed, and that she was the only one who could change her life, so she did. She went back to school and married someone much more suitable. Unfortunately her ex-boyfriend did not change. Eventually his rage destroyed him and he died a mysterious, violent death.

Five of Spades: Depression or Major Obstacles.
This card symbolizes depression and where it comes into play. There is much sadness and a feeling of hopelessness. This card means that you should take notice of what is lacking in your life and try to change it.

I told one woman who received this card in her fifth house that she was not enjoying herself, but she disagreed. It turned out that she tended to sit on the sidelines and watch others have a good time. She was investigating with her therapist the reasons why she never participated in any of the festivities she observed.

Six of Spades: Courage and a Strong Will.
This card shows that you need to have a final "say" on what is going on. It indicates that you have had some problems in your life that need to be reckoned with. This card calls for courage and is not for the slack-minded. You have a rare opportunity to fix what is wrong in your life and make it right—take advantage of it.

Seven of Spades: Taking Risk.
This card is about taking risks because you are at your limit. Usually it comes up in a reading when someone has had enough of a situation and is ready to make some changes. It is a self-realization card—one that hits you with the feeling that says: "If I want control of a situation, then only I can change it."

Eight of Spades: Immediate Change.
This card is regarded as the change card. It means that something inside of you—triggered either by your circumstances or your true will—is about to make you do something in an unorthodox manner. It is the type of card that makes a shy person find his or her voice or a loudmouth start to listen. The change is strong and empowering.

Nine of Spades: Radical Difference.
This is a stubborn card. It shows up for people who always believe they are right or who are unwilling to share. It also can mean that you are getting tired of the way your life has been going and you are considering how life would be with a radical change. Do not hold back; take the plunge.

Ten of Spades: Achievement Over Obstacles.
The ten of spades is an intense card and one that should never be taken lightly. This card means that life has been difficult for a long time, but now there is light at the end of the tunnel. Even though your journey has been difficult, you can see improvement. You have been diligent in working through difficulties to solve a problem and can now see relief from your effort. The ten of spades is about coming through a storm and accomplishing the impossible.

One client whom I saw over many years received this card a lot. She had been a high-school dropout who was working nights to pay her way through school. Eventually she graduated from a university with a four-year degree, much to everyone's amazement.

Face Cards

Jack of Spades: A Dark-haired, Dark-eyed Individual. Jacks of Spades are always young people who have dark hair and eyes. They tend to be quiet and sometimes sullen and do little to interact with the world around them. Some consider the people of this card antisocial, but this is not true. They are introverted and deep and can be moody but also profound. They tend to process a lot on their own and do not feel comfortable wearing their heart out on their sleeve.

Queen of Spades: A Dark-haired, Dark-eyed Woman. The Queen of Spades is always dark-haired and dark-eyed woman. She is self-assured, strong, and able to stand on her own two feet and make decisions—she definitely knows her own mind. Traditionally she is looked upon as a dark and jealous woman—someone who is to be avoided. I tend to look at this card as one who does not suffer fools gladly. This person is definitely someone you would want on your side.

King of Spades: A Dark-haired, Dark-eyed Man. This card signifies dark men with black to dark brown hair. They are always intense. Traditionally this card is a morally dark and unworthy individual, but I believe this is not true. The king of spades more often represents people who are reserved; they think about what they are going to say first. They have much on their mind, are deep in thought, and can be calculating.

In one reading, this card appeared in the first house for a woman. I told her I was surprised because I had not seen this king representing a female before. I told her that this card was so strong that she must be an unusually gifted and strong person to be this card. In fact, I told her, people probably think that her position is held by a man and are surprised that she is a woman. She was self-assured and said that I was right. She was the president of a large corporation and had worked her way up to the top. Only the king of spades could have made that climb; and people always asked her how she did it.

It's important to remember that face cards can be people of any race or color, even if some physical traits are mentioned as being connected with specific cards in the book. That is just how I was taught. Much depends on where one is reading and in what community. If one is reading in a culture where people look alike, then face shape is a deciding factor. "Hearts people" have heart shaped faces, "Diamonds people" have angular shaped faces, "Clubs people" have broad round shaped faces, and "Spades people" have square shaped faces. Use your intuition!.

CHAPTER 3

The Small Star Spread

The Small Star spread is a beginner's spread. It is a wonderful way to see how the cards interact with each other and a good way to get an immediate feel for the cards and for giving readings.

My grandmother taught me the cards using this spread because I could see how the cards related to one another and could get quick answers to my questions. I have used this method to teach others how to use the cards and, since it provides immediate results, it is an enjoyable way to learn.

The Small Star spread provides information on what is happening now in your life. It shows the recent past and the soon-to-be future. This is not a reading for seeing how the next week or month will turn out. You can use this spread daily to see how everything is going. One of my friends calls it the reality check layout.

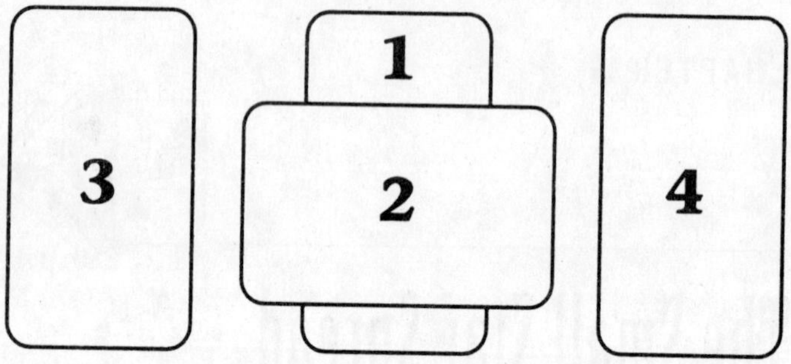

Fig. 1– Small Star spread

To begin the Small Star spread, shuffle the cards until you feel that they are really mixed up and you are ready. (Preparing the cards this way is called centering yourself with the cards.) Next, cut the cards three times.

Pull the first four cards from the deck. Put the first card face up vertically on the table in front of you. Put the second card horizontally over the first card. Put the third card on the left side of the crossed cards and the fourth card on the right side of the crossed cards.

The first card is where you are now. The second card is what is covering you; that is, the biggest immediate influence. The third card is the immediate past, the fourth is the immediate future.

To read the cards, refer to chapter 2, "The Meanings of the Cards."

Sample Reading: Pat

This reading was for Pat, a neighbor of mine with whom I had coffee frequently and who was waiting to hear some good news about a job.

Sophia: This is a simple way to read the cards. It is a great way to start out in the morning and see how your day is going to go. I find it fun and entertaining to use, besides being accurate. The first card is where you are now and you have the five of spades there. You are feeling somewhat depressed about your current situation.

Pat: This is true. Not having a job really gets me down.

Sophia: Over you is the king of clubs. It is your husband since he has direct influence over you and he fits the physical description.

Pat: He gives me grief about finding work, but I don't want to work just any job. I'm going to hold out to get what I want this time.

Sophia: The third card is the nine of spades. In the past you have found it difficult to change and have been stubborn.

Pat: Boy, is that ever true!

Sophia: Good news in the future, you have the ace of diamonds. It looks like all will change for the better. You may get that job after all. Aces are wild so it might be sudden.

Pat: That would be wonderful news.

Pat did get her job. In fact, the next day she was called in for an interview. The job was what she had been looking for and the company hired her immediately.

Sample Reading: Student

This next reading was done for a student in a class I taught.

Sophia: Pull four cards. Lay the first card down, then put another card on top of that, then put the third card on the left side of the crossed cards and the fourth card on the right.

Student: What does it mean? Okay, let me try. The first card is where I am at now, right? With the eight of diamonds, that means I am in a good place. Money is good. True. With the five of hearts over it, it would mean I'll get love. The third is the queen of spades so that is someone I know, a woman; and the fourth card is the ten of diamonds. I think that means something good. Big money, right? How did I do?

Sophia: Very good for the first time. Here, let me try. You're right. You're in a good place with the eight of diamonds. Your dreams are finally starting to come true. Anything you want is coming your way now. In fact, with the five of hearts covering you, you're going out and having a ball—I bet with a special friend. I would also say that this is something that was unexpected and you're having a great time doing what you want. What happened, did you win the lottery?

Student: Close…a sudden windfall.

Sophia: The card in your past is a woman who is dark, maybe in character. I find it interesting that she is in your past and your other cards denote fun and success. Either she is someone who you don't care too much about or she left you some money, some kind of estate.

Student: Bingo. She was an aunt who has spent the last ten years in a nursing home. When her estate was closed, we found out a surprise. She was very, very, rich. I am her only living relative, so I got everything.

Sophia: Lucky you! With the ten of diamonds you'll have a great time taking advantage of all that is yours.

Student: I plan to!

As you can see, the Small Star spread is an easy way to learn and enjoy the cards. I recommend that you practice this layout and become good at it before you move to the other spreads.

CHAPTER 4

The Wheel of Life Spread: A Reading Spread Based on the Zodiac

This is the spread that I use the most often, and therefore it is the one I will spend the most time explaining. This is, in fact, the spread that my grandmother emphasized for me, though she used several others that I will mention later. I am attracted to this particular pattern for card reading because I am also interested in astrology. As I have used the spread over the years, I have come to depend on it more and have found new meaning in it every time. You do not need to know much about astrology to use the Wheel of Life spread. In fact, all you have to know is that this spread corresponds with the Zodiac and that the twelve places to put the cards correspond to the twelve signs (houses) of the Zodiac.

After instructions on how to use the spread, you will find a short explanation of what the twelve houses mean. Chapter 5 outlines the meanings of the cards as used in this spread, and chapter 6 provides sample readings so you can see how the cards in this spread all come together.

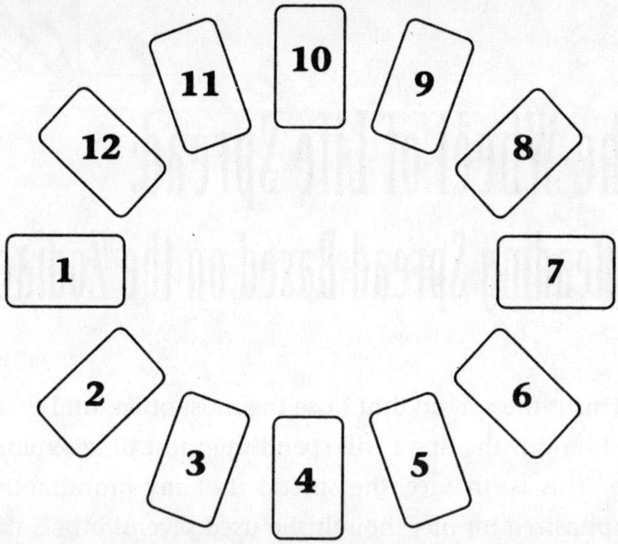

Fig. 2– The Wheel of Life spread

To begin the Wheel of Life spread, shuffle the cards three times (or have the person who is getting the reading do so). Cut the cards into three piles with your left hand. The person getting the reading puts the three piles back into one pile. Take the pile of cards and lay out twelve of them in a circle, counterclockwise (see the Wheel of Life spread illustration).

You will read the meanings of the cards as they relate to the houses that they are in, each house being one of the twelve positions corresponding to an astrological sign. Chapter 2 listed the general meanings of the cards. However, chapter 5 lists the meaning of each of the fifty-two cards in each of the twelve houses. Use the meanings in chapter 5 when using the Wheel of Life spread (use the general meanings in chapter 2 for the other spreads mentioned in this book).

You'll find that reading each meaning of each card as it sits in each house is easy. You just look in the right places and read. It is more difficult, however, to see how the cards relate to one another. A good reader will pick up the subtle nuances and make the reading more personable.

When laying out the cards, check to see where they physically land. Do any point to each other? It is important not just what the card means but, when you are laying out the cards, how they happen to fall. If a face card is pointing to a number card, that means that either this person has direct power over you or your decisions in life are greatly influencing this person. If any cards are touching, there is a greater influence between these cards than any others in the circle. This is the most significant place in your life, where you are the most affected; check here to see what is going on or what is driving you. These cards may indicate how you react and what needs to be worked on.

For example, if the queen of spades is in the eighth house, she would probably be a lover and/or mentor. If the card was pointed down to the seventh house, it would mean that she was a partner in a business or marriage; if it was pointed to the ninth house, it might be a teacher or someone you wanted to impress. If the card is not touching any other cards, it would be someone in your life who is not directly involved and may be somewhat distant from things. Read through chapter 6 to see exactly how a reading should be done using the Wheel of Life spread. Remember, use your intuition!

The Twelve Houses of the Zodiac and the Cards

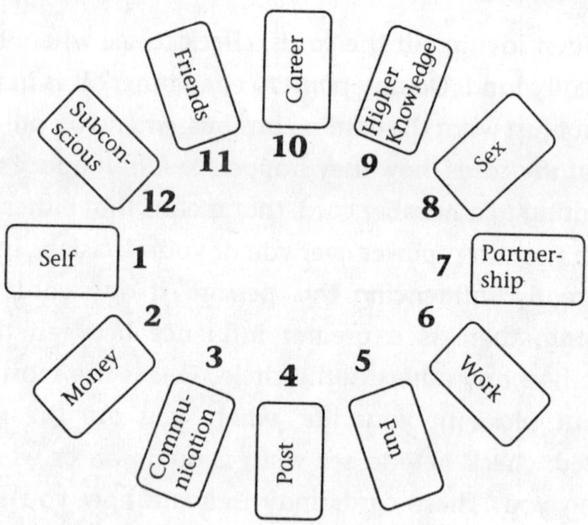

Fig. 3– The twelve houses as they relate to the Wheel of Life spread

The houses are divided into twelve separate zones with different meanings. Picture a wheel with twelve spokes. When you interpret the cards, this system shows you how the cards are affected. It is not just what the card means, but how the card plays itself out. For example, a face card means that a person who meets a certain description will have a certain character. Depending on where that card lands, this tells you what type of person they are and/or how they are related to you. If a face card (say the king of hearts) lands in the seventh house, it would represent a blond-haired, blue-eyed man who is your partner. In cartomancy, the wheel layout is called an astrological spread. Any good astrology book will help you learn the cards as they relate to the houses much more in depth. An astrology book will also tell you about the houses and what they signify. Following is a brief explanation of the houses in an astrological spread.

First House: This connects with the planet Mars and the sign of Aries; it is the house of beginnings. It represents your ego; how you fit into the world and your mask or how others see you. What is the first impression you give? Is your approach cautious, like the two of clubs, or do you appear as a hopeless romantic, like the five of hearts?

The first house gives you clues about how you appear to others and insight on your behavior at the time. If you are having problems that you cannot solve or are suffering from the "Why me?" syndrome, the card in this house could give you some answer as to why things do not seem to go your way. It will also show the mask or the cover that we all use to comfort ourselves; the mask we project to the world. It is the way we cope and understand our surroundings.

The first house is the beginning of establishing personal identity. In the case of the cards, it is what is surrounding us; it is the most important opportunity, person, or risk facing us at this time. It is how you deal with a particular situation. In the case of the ten of hearts, you are blessed with a good fortune and have a rare chance to move forward with your goals. If you do not take advantage of the situations around you, you can strike out.

Any face card you get would represent you. In some readings, I have seen a face card signify another person; that happens, however, only if the other person is someone who is always on your mind, much like an obsessive love. A face card can also be a person whose identity is so closely related to you that you are having a difficult time seeing who you are for yourself. This is not the best place to be—it means you are losing connection with who you really are.

Basically, the first house represents you and the most important things in your life. It represents how you approach others. In a reading, the simplest idea is to remember that this card is you or your current state of being. If you are reading someone else's card, then it is that person's most important direction. If the card is a spade, you project gloom and doom. Diamonds show that social status, charisma, and money are headed your way.

Clubs reveal you are driven; you have intense goals and you want to achieve. Hearts show that you ooze love and lushness—very Venusian—so others are drawn to you.

Second House: This is the house of possessions or belonging; it is the house you look at to see how someone relates to money. Lower number cards in this house suggest that you do not have adequate funds and that money can be a major problem. Lack of money has stopped you from enjoying your life, especially if that card is a club or spade.

In a reading I was giving to a single woman, a face card appeared here, which indicated she shared her money with another person. I asked her who she shared her money with. Even though she was middle-aged and had an excellent job as an librarian, she lived with her father (she owned the home they lived in). Her father completely controlled the purse strings—she gave him the money and he paid their bills. This was not the happiest situation for her, but she felt she had no control. If you find a face card in this circle; you either share your resources or the other person controls the money. It is more a feeling of powerlessness then anything else.

This house is also your resources; it covers real estate, finances, gardening, and food. Mainly, though, it covers what you own or what you feel is rightfully yours. It can also indicate loss of possessions. In some readings, it is clear that someone has lost his or her home or one's home is undergoing major remodeling. Many times, people have enough money but they do not feel like it is enough. Usually a spade gives the feeling of not having enough, and clubs show that you work very hard for what is yours. Diamonds show money is not much of a problem, and hearts reveal that it is not much of a problem either, though saving might be. This house can also give you insights into ways to increase your fortune—usually from a business out of your home. It can also be a feeling of being in touch with your surroundings and a love of gardening. If you want to gain insight into eating habits, this is the best place to look. Spades or clubs would be a dieter, and hearts or diamonds would be a tendency to overindulge.

The easiest way to remember the second house is to think about resources for both yourself and others. This is the area where you set out to accomplish what you want on the material plane and to achieve your goals to make your life more comfortable. Spades are discomfort, clubs are work, hearts are enjoyment, and diamonds are making money at home.

Third House: This is the house of communication; it also represents teaching and writing. It is the most beneficial when viewed in your readings with the idea that in order to create or think you must put everything together in a manner that makes sense to yourself and others. This is the beginning of self-expression.

One way to imagine what this house represents is to think about being a teenager. With a teenager (or even with some adults), the need to express yourself so others understand what you are saying is very strong—only sometimes others do not understand what you are going through, especially your parents. You try many ways to have people hear your voice—yelling, screaming, acting out—but nothing seems to work. As a result, you start to develop self-realization or the reality of having to communicate your ideas and actions coherently. Then you look at how you can best express yourself. This is the start of communication to others in a manner that gets your ideas out; this is the beginning of the third house.

In a reading, look at what is surrounding this house to see who you are trying to reach out to and effectively communicate with. With spades, your voice is not heard; clubs are saying that you need to try another way of communicating; diamonds show you could earn money through teaching or through writing; hearts show that others are moved by what you say. Also, look at the influences of your writing and speaking.

In a reading I gave to one woman, she had the two of spades in the third house. She told me that nothing seemed to click, others did not listen to her. It was obvious that she needed to take more time in getting her point across (the emphasis here is her point) and that persistence would help her be understood. So it is with the third house; remember, communication is only as good as you make it.

Fourth House: This is home; it can either be the home in which you were raised or your current home. Many times, it is how you feel about your home and your emotions centering around your home. In a card reading, this house can indicate a move or change in one's home. A face card would be a signal that either the person shares a home with another or that they will have a visitor fitting the description of the card.

Many times, though, a face card will show that the person shares a home with another and that frequently the home is not their own. I have seen this with roommates or, more commonly, with a house guest who has worn out their welcome. In one reading in Tokyo, a man was proclaiming that his home "didn't feel like his." He said he had no say in the household. It was clear he had moved in with his wife into her apartment, and they both had a difficult time in deciding what belonged where. Later, they looked for an apartment that would fit both their needs—which was no easy task in Tokyo where apartments are hard to find.

This house can also mean the past and trying to get over some past hurt that has prevented you from living a more meaningful life. In the case of spades, it can be either sadness in the home or the loss of home. It is the idea that your home is not what makes you happy. With clubs, work within the home is commonly indicated in readings for people who have done extensive redecorating or are about to redecorate. Diamonds can reveal the possibility to earn money in your home. If you have ever thought of opening up a home business, this is the best time to get the wheels in motion, especially if the ten of diamonds appears. Hearts show much love in the home; either the person is a homebody and enjoys that or the person has a wonderful family life. When I see a heart card here, I tell my clients that their home life is good (depending on the number; 2 is good, 10 is excellent).

Fifth House: This is the house of fun, entertainment, and pleasure; it is the house to look at to see what the person enjoys. This house also represents creativity. What is it that we like to do to make our lives more creative? How do we harness the pleasure of making something new and finishing up projects that result in a creative process? It's all here.

This is also the house of children. People who desire a child or have questions about a child should look here. The eleventh house is the place to look to find out what makes a child who he or she is—the actual beginning of creating a child is here in the fifth house (once again, pleasure).

Hearts would reinforce pleasure as well as reveal someone who could create something worthwhile. In the case of Spades, this person would be blocked from doing any art. He or she probably has few creative ideas or is stuck doing something that does not make them happy. Frequently this could be money issues. Clubs show that something is a lot of work, or work is pleasure. For individuals who have friends at work, they may take up most of their free time. It might also mean that the person is so goal-oriented that only through work can he or she find true joy. Diamonds mean having fun wherever you go and it is easy to make friends who have money. If you ever wanted to cash in with your art, now is the time. Face cards represent actual people you would be spending time with. It is either someone with whom you enjoy an evening out or someone who is your party friend.

It is best to find a balance with the fifth house. Some people party so much that it is not clear to them when the party is over; there is no fun in overindulgence to the point where others or alcohol and drugs take over. This house is also a good place to look at creative blocks. A frequently asked question is, "I am having no fun in life; what can I do to enjoy myself more?" The fifth house will give clues as to how this person can enjoy life more.

Sixth House: This is the house of work; it is the responsibilities of life and shows we all need to be filled with a purpose. It shows our duties to others as well as to ourselves. It covers work inside and outside the home, pets, and health. The objective to keep in mind is what keeps someone focused and what his or her key skills.are. Many times, we all have wondered what we are best at doing, how we can best make a living, how we can best use our skills and abilities to achieve what we want, how we can find our life's work. The sixth house holds the key to all of this.

If you have spades here, you have many problems with work, and frequently you are underemployed or unemployed. Spades sometimes indicate that you are in danger of losing your job. If clubs, then work is difficult and either you have too much responsibility or you are under constant strain at your workplace. Hearts show you are on the right track to the kind of work that you enjoy. Occasionally it is a volunteer position that brings great happiness to yourself as well as to others. Diamonds show that work is important to you and others respect and like you at your job.

The face cards are people who you have a feeling of duty toward. Either they are your boss, coworker, or perhaps a friend or family member who needs your help. The important object here is that you are in a position to help someone less fortunate or demanding of you and so you should give in gracefully. All face cards also represent real people who need your attention. Work to help others make transitions in this house.

The sixth house is also for health. This is where you look for your general health. If it is a spade, expect minor to major illness depending on the number (2 being a little ill, 10 being quite sick). Clubs show that you need to work on your health. You are long overdue to take care of yourself and this neglect could bring health problems. Hearts show that you have a good attitude toward your health and that you are optimistic. Diamonds reveal a feeling of strength and energy.

Seventh House: What is it that makes us click with another person? Is it animal attraction, desire, loneliness, love? Whatever the answer, we need to find a way to bring people closer and develop relationships with others. This is the house of partnership and usually indicates marriage—but it can also symbolize business partnerships or any type of fifty-fifty relationship.

For major relationship questions, look here in a reading. It is where you will find the most important relationship going on; look around at the cards next to it to see contributing factors to the relationship. What is it that makes it work or not work? It is a great way to see another person's point of view.

Frequently, clients ask about love and marriage and this is the first place to look in a reading to answer those types of questions. If the card is a spade, relationships are not the easiest for this person. Either they are mad at another or loneliness is their companion. This can be true in a relationship where communication is poor. It is important to continue to look at this in the respect that the cards are giving insight into the person's love life. Spades say you are having serious problems in your relationship, not a great time for either person. Clubs show much work on the relationship; both may need a break from each other. Any break would be short-term, usually just a day or so. Clubs also show how we love. Many times, clubs indicate a shallow relationship that needs fixing. Hearts are love, love, love; romance and marriage are here to stay. Diamonds show a great time for business deals with a loved one.

Face cards indicate the actual looks of people in your life much more than in some of the other houses. A spade is a dark-haired, dark-eyed person. Clubs reveal a brunette, brown to hazel eyes. Hearts show a very fair, blond person with blue or green eyes. A diamond person has light hair and light to dark eyes. Never in a reading have I heard someone say about a face card, "This is nobody I know." They all say the same thing: "Oh, that's —!" The seventh house is how we love and who we love—an important factor to remember in a reading.

Eighth House: Traditionally this is the house of sex and death; it is the sexual bond that holds us to others. In a reading, this is where you would find out about a lover or someone you are attracted to. Animal magnetism is the overpowering drive here.

Classically, this is also the house of death; it can mean that someone will pass on, but mostly it is the giving up of yourself for the bigger picture. Creating a piece of art that survives the passage of time is a good example. It is the idea that in order to get you must give up part of yourself for a different way of being. Self-sacrifice is indicated here. It also includes other people's money, taxes, legal contracts, and lawyers. This is a great house to look at to get the bigger picture in a reading and to find out what it is that people need to do to make a more fulfilling life.

In a reading I gave to one man, he had a spade card in the eighth house. He wanted to collect from an individual he thought owed him money. It was clear that the money was not my client's and he just felt that through association with this individual he should get the money. When this fact was pointed out, I said, "Just because your ex-associate has gone on to earn more money than you does not mean that you are entitled to the same amount." He argued with me for some time that he should get the money because he wanted it, but I had to point out to him that desire does not make it so. This is the key to the eighth house; wishing on a star for what you want will not necessarily mean it will come to you. Sometimes in life you must take a stand or sacrifice. Through the card reading, the man was able to see that his former associate had to risk to earn money after this man had bailed out, thinking he did not want to take a risk. His friend made money for his trouble; my client's mistake was thinking he could get something for nothing. You cannot.

Spades here show difficulties with others; it is not a good time to take a risk. Clubs reveal that you need to resolve issues with others; look over any fine print in a contract. Diamonds reveal that someone could make you an offer that is hard to refuse. Hearts show good sex; others find you very desirable. Face cards represent a sexual partner or someone you are very attracted to.

Ninth House: Higher knowledge, travel to foreign countries, new experiences—all are ninth house matters. Look here to see the future in a reading and what the best possibilities are for expansion. What would benefit you the most? A long trip to another country to experience a different culture? Courses to develop a new interest or expand the skills you already have? Whatever you decide, this house will help you realize what the best course of action is to obtain new heights. This is definitely an active house and it is wise to take some steps to achieve what you want. It is good to look at this as the house of goals—what do you believe in? What are your thoughts on philosophy or religion? Your belief system could be changed and it is important that you have insight into what you believe is the truth. The ninth house is for truth seekers and for those who are questioning themselves and others. When someone comes to have a reading and asks the question, "What should I do in the future?" I look here to find the best course of action.

Spades show that it is not the best time to start anything new or to go on a trip. Clubs show you need to work on developing yourself. When I see a club here, I usually take this as a sign to start reading more books on thoughts and theory. Diamonds show that it is a great time to go back to school or travel. Hearts show that anything you expand on or learn will help you develop ideas that will last a lifetime. Face cards indicate that you either know or will meet someone who will have a profound effect on you. Many times, this person will be a teacher or a spiritual leader. The ninth house lets you look beyond the horizon.

Tenth House: This is the house of goals, long-term aspirations, and careers. This is not like the sixth house, which is more duty and work. The tenth house is career—what is it that fuels your drive and ambition? What kind of work is it that allows you to be paid, to be yourself? Asking questions about the type of work reveals whether this is the correct vocation or if it is the place where you should begin to work now.

Many times in readings, people come to get a glimpse of their career future; they want to know where they would be the most successful or make the maximum amount of money with their skills. The tenth house gives insight into this. This house is one of the more difficult to deal with because we often find differences between what we want to be and what we are doing now. If you want to see the forces behind a dream job, this is where you would look.

One woman I read for wanted to be a writer; she believed her talent was as good as a famous novelist who would win prestigious awards even though she had never written anything. I asked her how she knew that. "I just know," she replied. It could be true, but it does not mean anything unless she produces. Her card did not show this because the tenth house reveals what you actually are doing now and some future goals. Usually, a card reading shows what is going on at that moment. Remember, the cards are good for only about two weeks—unless one has a lower number card that would indicate a new beginning. The woman was wrong; she was not a novelist. The cards pointed out that she needed to look at her career much more realistically so she could find direction in her life.

Spades show you need to develop a realistic view of your work. Clubs indicate much career work ahead of you, fine-tuning your skills. Diamonds show a promotion or raise at work. Hearts indicate you love what you do, and should keep up the good work. Face cards are people you work for or with.

Eleventh House: This is the house of friends, children, creative ideas, and innovative thinking; encouraging energy is prominent here. What type of friends you attract is what matters here; the type of people with whom you spend most of the time reflects who you are. As they say, "Birds of a feather flock together." If you chose your friends unwisely, you tend to go nowhere; you hang around with no particular destination. Choose wisely and you will enjoy yourself and others.

With any face card, look at what is surrounding it. The surrounding cards will tell you what type of friends you have. Almost every time a face card lands here, whomever I give the reading to identifies this person as a best friend. How they interact would be shown by the cards around them. Once in a while, a face card may reflect children. When this happens, the mother or father always says, "My daughter (or son) is my best friend." This is the key more to the personality of the children and the relationship; usually the children are teenagers or young adults. They are unusually close with their parent or parents. Many times I have seen a face card representing a child in single-parent families.

Creative ideas are also highlighted in the eleventh house, but it is not the best house to look at if you want to see how it will work out. This house is more centered on the idea itself. What is it that makes everything click? High tech is also prominent here; computers, software, movies, and the Internet are all connected with this house.

The eleventh house is where you look to see overall future influence. Hidden talents are often located here as well as people you are trying to influence, such as mentors or people in power who can move your future to higher heights. It is important to be careful with interpreting any face cards here. Carefully ask "who" and "how" of these people. Also, the eleventh house covers publishing and books. Look here for anyone who writes or has thought about being a writer.

Spades indicate that any major project should be put on hold; think all the way through an idea, do not act on impulse. Clubs show that the person is working on long-term plans; it is a great time to evaluate dreams and what the person really wants out of life. Diamonds show that ideas could pay off; think big! Hearts mean that one should follow the heart and go for what is really wanted and needed in life.

Twelfth House: Here we are in the land of mystery; this is the house of the subconscious. What is it that makes us cope in times of need? If everything has not been going your way and life is stressful, look here to find what is really hampering you. As many have said before, we are our own worst enemy. This can be so true; we can stand in our own way and prevent ourselves from doing what we want. Traditionally this is the house of leaping into fantasy and overindulgence with alcohol or drugs. It can certainly relate to anything that is harmful if overdone and used as an escape. It is important to use anything in moderation when involved in the twelfth house.

One young man who came for a reading was upset that everything was not like in TV shows. He thought that if he bought advertised items that he too could have a happier life. It was clear that he watched so much television that it was like a drug; it ruled his life. He equated television with reality. I told him to turn off the TV and get a job. He did and started to make friends (and his mother was happy, too).

The twelfth house is where you look for blocks in your life, either by your own reality or by finding what it is that stops you from reaching your potential. Many times in a reading, spades here mean a person is depressed.

Clubs indicate that one is involved with a direction in life that he or she does not really like. Diamonds show a person is optimistic about the future and everything is going better. Hearts show a deep appreciation for spiritual matters. Face cards represent people on the mind, either a lover or an enemy. Sometimes it is a person you can never get off your mind.

Most of all, the twelfth house reveals spiritual growth and advancement. It includes all the beautiful mysteries of life. Look at the twelfth house as the end of the karmic wheel. When finishing the reading, tie in all that you said before with this house. It is where one checks to see what the cards, overall, are trying to tell you or what the lesson is that one should learn from all this. Check the twelfth house to fill in any missing piece. In a reading, I refer to this last house as the place of advice because the reading has finished and you can now say what you want to, either to yourself or the individual you read for.

Reading the cards is like any other psychic activity; you should put yourself into a comfortable and "open" state of mind. When you shuffle, do so as unconsciously possible. Do the same when you lay the cards out in a circle, keep your mind on the question and not on how you lay the cards down. If you do this right, it won't be neat, but you'll learn much from the "chance" way you did things.

CHAPTER 5

Card Meanings for the Wheel of Life Spread

Use the information in this chapter to find out the meaning of the cards in the Wheel of Life spread. For all other spreads, use the card meanings found in chapter 2.

♥ Hearts

Ace of Hearts: An Overpowering Love.

First house: Not for the faint of heart! Love and romance surrounds you. You have a certain beauty and elegance that others admire and are attracted to. You can accomplish anything now if you want to.

Second house: A great time to develop and do what you love. Push ahead in romance, creativity, and any earthly desires.

Third house: Reconnecting with an old flame will make you both feel like kids again; have fun talking about the good old days.

Fourth house: Love in the family and in the home. Others come to visit you because you make them feel like part of the family.

Fifth house: Spending time and hanging around in your favorite spot, you could start a chance meeting with a stranger. You have much in common; be open to any chance encounters.

Sixth house: This is an office fling that could be much more than you both bargained for. Be cautious so as not to cause either of you problems in the future.

Seventh house: Either the beginning of a long love affair or you and your partner rediscover the love you have for each other. This is a good place to put the ace of hearts in a love spell.

Eighth house: Sex and passion in such an intense way that you almost lose yourselves in a night of brilliant lovemaking. Hold on tight!

Ninth house: If you have ever wanted to go on a vacation that you would never forget, you may want to take off somewhere with a certain somebody soon.

Tenth house: Your personal power is very strong right now. Go after all long-term goals and desires. Yes, your dreams could be realized.

Eleventh house: A friendship turns into more with this card. For a period of about three weeks, this card turned up for me in readings, always in the same place. The relationship developed into much more and we've now been married for ten years.

Twelfth house: Dreams of loved ones are particularly psychic right now. Write down in a journal what you dream; it will prove to be shocking at a later date.

Two of Hearts: A Sweet Encounter.

First house: Everything flows to you very easily now. People see you as a very pleasant person. You are asked to participate in many different types of events. If there is anyone or anyplace you are thinking of visiting, now is a good time. You are received cordially and with respect.

Second house: Money grows steadily and any investments you make will prosper. Remember, though, that the key word with the two of hearts is *small*. Any increase should be in a small amount, but it is also sure to grow slowly over time This is a great card for gardeners; it's time to plant seedlings or hard-to-grow plants.

Third house: Letters are answered, telephone calls are made, and any kind of communication flows smoothly.

You can reach others with the sound of your voice. Good card for telephone solicitors and chatty friends.

Fourth house: Family and home life are relaxing and harmonious and this is a good time to pursue hobbies at home. Any project that you start at this time will bring you much happiness.

Fifth house: You are either entertaining on a small scale in your home or helping others with parties and/or plans. This card means that your party will be a definite success. Others will comment on your skill as a host or hostess.

Sixth house: Your work is easy right now, everything seems to glide off your desk. Relationships at work are compatible. There is a friendship that has not always been that helpful, but now it starts to improve. Health is good.

Seventh house: Relationships with marriage and business partners are easy right now. Communication seems to be easier and a general feeling of warmth surrounds you and your loved one.

Eighth house: Expect a small unexpected present. It could be simple praise from someone you wanted to impress in the past or it might be a card from an admirer.

Ninth house: A short weekend trip would benefit you greatly and will be easy to take now. A trip to the country will make you feel fresh and renewed. You will at least do something new.

Tenth house: Career and school are very enjoyable right now. You have much more social time at both. Rewards follow.

Eleventh house: Your friends and you have some memorable times, make plans to see old friends.

Twelfth house: You are having pleasant dreams and are in a good mental state; this positive attitude will cover you.

Three of Hearts: Influencing Others.

First house: Many different types of people are attracted to you. You are in an optimistic mood and are feeling positive about yourself. A strong sense of self helps you to know your life's direction.

Second house: Money matters are going stronger for you. Ask for a raise, this is a favorable time. You may be asked to work some overtime.

Third house: Contacting a cousin or siblings you have not seen in a while brings up many happy memories for you both.

Fourth house: Good time to finish that long overdue scrapbook; start to organize your memories and maybe your photo album. Consider contacting loved ones from the past.

Fifth house: You kick up your heels and laugh and laugh. Life is one pleasant get-together after another. Friends are featured prominently.

Sixth house: You make a new friend at work; you both consider volunteering for a committee.

Seventh house: You and your significant other spend time conversing about what truly matters to you both.

Eighth house: A friend has more than friendship on his or her mind. These romantic intentions are very noble. You say yes.

Ninth house: Read that book your best friend has recommended. You gain great insight into each other.

Tenth house: New coworker or friend shows you new ways to increase your money and knowledge; seize this chance.

Eleventh house: Friendship is renewed. Spend time with old and new friends and be truly honest about how you feel; the insight you gain will last a lifetime.

Twelfth house: You are feeling and thinking positive, loving thoughts about life; others ask what your secret is.

Four of Hearts: Realistic Love.

First house: You are starting to see below the surface and how you appear to your loved ones. Also you are in such a good mood you wonder what other people's problems are when they do not smile back.

Second house: A close look at each other's tastes in fashion and home furnishing. Both of you wonder about the other; can you live with someone whose ideas of accessories and lifestyles are so different from yours?

Third house: You both agree on everything; it seems too good to be true and you wonder if your partner is going along with you or if you both really see eye-to-eye.

Fourth house: There is love and coziness in the home, but you are a little restless. You are wondering how others live. I have seen this card in readings when someone watches too much TV and has a fantasy about movie stars.

Fifth house: More, more, more! Not content with what you have, you are trying to find a creative inspiration. This is a wonderful card for those in the artistic field.

Sixth house: You are called upon to nurture another person or an injured animal. It brings you deep satisfaction to be of service to others.

Seventh house: Everything has been going well in your relationship. This card is a signal saying it is important not to let things slide. Send your beloved a Valentine's Day card on a day that is not February 14.

Eighth house: This is a warm, caring relationship; you both are very attentive to each other's needs. Some are jealous of your closeness—who cares about them?

Ninth house: You take up a new subject, something that you love and have never developed. In one reading, a client got this card and I asked her what she had always wanted to do. She said she wanted to learn sign language, even though she had no family member or friend who was deaf. She felt strongly about it. She soon started to learn to sign.

Tenth house: You are doing well at work and are very capable; it seems that almost everything you try now is second nature. You might feel that you are all thumbs, but you do not appear this way to others.

Eleventh house: You and another have been friends for years; it seems that when one thinks of the other, each of you gives the other a call. You help each other in many ways both small and large.

Twelfth house: A good attitude goes a long way. Your happy-go-lucky ways rub off on others. A great sense of humor is indicated with this card.

Five of Hearts: Great Fortune.

First house: Good luck and radiant health surround you. You feel vibrant and others ask you if you have lost weight or changed your looks in any way. Tell them it is your inner glow.

Second house: If you ever wanted to gamble on the stock market, try now. This is a great card for risk taking. Use this card in any money spell to ensure wealth.

Third house: Good time to start thinking of anything you might want to create at a later date. Any ideas would be good money makers in the future.

Fourth house: Children and parents are very important right now; you need to spend time with both. They tend to be very generous with you at this time.

Fifth house: Creativity is featured; dust off any old projects and finish them. In the past this card could have been blocking you.

Sixth house: You seem to be working less and making more money. How do you manage that? Your health is excellent; you motivate your peers to exercise.

Seventh house: Love, romance, passion are all here for you and your partner to enjoy. This is a wonderful time of exploration for you both. You discover yourselves through each other.

Eighth house: You may receive money through legal channels Anything in this category ensures that you are the winner. In card spells, be careful, you may win your lawsuit, but you might not like how you win.

Ninth house: Take that exotic trip that you always dreamed about, even if it is only for a weekend; romance and love await you. This card is especially strong in this house. Use it in a card spell to realize your long-term dreams. Any student of astrology will notice the connection with Jupiter here.

Tenth house: If you ever thought of changing careers, now is the time. Make sure any changes you make involve teaching, travel, high tech, or working with people or small animals. This card guarantees success!

Eleventh house: You and your friends or partner have some award-winning ideas; put them to use and you will have amazing good luck.

Twelfth house: Write down your dreams; you have some successful images coming through—use them.

Six of Hearts: Long-Term Good Luck.

The six of hearts is a little stronger than the five. While the five of hearts is good luck, the six is more good luck that has been around for a while—only you may not have been using it to your benefit. This card is telling you to take notice of what is going on. If you really have your heart set on anything, you should go for it. This a great card for going that extra mile for something that you really want.

First house: You are feeling pretty cocky right now, although some might see this as aggressive behavior even if you do not. This is a wonderful card for those who are self-employed.

Second house: You plan on spreading out your investments; do not spread your money too thin. Keep on top with any investment.

Third house: Your journal writing is paying off; those thoughts and feelings you had are now starting to form into something more concrete.

Fourth house: Family and home continue to be wonderful; you start to spend time in the kitchen trying out new recipes.

Fifth house: If you only played around with the idea of being in theater or some kind of performing art, this is your chance. You are in a good place to take creative risks.

Sixth house: Health is very good; be sure to take advantage of any diet you may encounter. Use your energy to get the job done.

Seventh house: You and your partner have been in good spirits for a while; take this time to enjoy each other.

Eighth house: You will be receiving attention from an old lover or a message that will give you a new direction.

Ninth house: Good time to take a new class and develop what you already know and become more of an expert.

Tenth house: Arrange a business meeting or party with your coworkers; you will learn much about office politics.

Eleventh house: Spend some alone time with a special friend. Catch up with the past; it will turn out to be crucial.

Twelfth house: Act on any insight you have to past problems and dilemmas. Do it now!

Seven of Hearts: Reunites People from the Past.

First house: You can attract much attention right now; this is a good card for actors and actresses, or just show-offs. You could land a major role.

Second house: A romantic encounter with someone in finances, such as a banker, real estate agent, or broker. You get more than you bargained for.

Third house: A family friend wants more from you. It is your call, but watch your step.

Fourth house: Family members are very affectionate. Some could get a little close for comfort; don't be afraid to ask for more space.

Fifth house: An old lover or a potential new lover you know wants to ask you out for an evening of fun—oh, forbidden fruit!

Sixth house: Your boss or coworker has more on his or her mind than you might think or, if you work with the public, a customer pursues you.

Seventh house: After all these months and years, you and a special friend have time for each other. Use this time wisely; it will not last forever.

Eighth house: A sexual encounter with an old acquaintance stirs up long-forgotten feelings. Should you or shouldn't you?

Ninth house: A hidden familiar getaway—perhaps a restaurant or cafe. You have warm feelings beckoning you to enjoy this old spot once again.

Tenth house: You are renewing an old, long-forgotten artistic skill that brings you great pleasure.

Eleventh house: Your friendship could turn to more if you become closer; this card tells you that you have a good chance.

Twelfth house: You have many secret animal passions about to be unleashed. Wow! Some wild dreams as well.

Eight of Hearts: An Intense Relationship.

First house: You see yourself in terms of a relationship. This card is normally seen in the readings of people who say, "My husband (or wife) and I believe..." or "We think...". It is a "royal we" card; not so independent.

Second house: Your money is tied up with another individual. You both make decisions regarding transactions.

Third house: Any way you want to influence another person in another city—through direct mail, faxes, telephone calls—now is the time to start.

Fourth house: Wonderful time to move or redecorate your home. You and your family finally agree what to save or toss in your home.

Fifth house: You and your significant lover rekindle your love for each other; use this card in a card spell for that heart-extra push.

Sixth house: Your health is excellent; a great time to start enjoying a new sport, especially one that involves risk.

Seventh house: You and your partner become closer than you have in years; you discover something new in the relationship.

Eighth house: Something unexpected drops in your lap! If you want to receive a gift or a very nice present, use this card in a card spell.

Ninth house: You and a close associate have a remarkable meeting of the minds; you both finally agree on everything.

Tenth house: If you take a second honeymoon now, you both will end up much more in sync with each other.

Eleventh house: You and your boss seem to be able to agree on something key. Use this card to influence others in a card spell.

Twelfth house: You can persuade others to think like you do, and you should do so now. Use it in card spells to gain power.

Nine of Hearts: An Intelligent Fling.

First house: You are thinking ahead and project an attitude of authority. Others come and ask you complicated questions.

Second house: A good combination of heart and feelings; you are able to put the two together to come up with creative solutions.

Third house: If you want to spend more time writing and reading, this is a fantastic card. For poets and writers, your inspiration couldn't be better.

Fourth house: Use this time to be creative; this is the time to show a younger person how to make something new. Good card for those involved with children.

Fifth house: Like minds work together, you both agree on almost everything. "Two-of-a-kind" is the key idea here.

Sixth house: If you ever wanted a pet, this is the time to get one. You could possibly even have one choose you.

Seventh house: You are analyzing your relationship and finding out that maybe you do not have it so bad. You make some decisions about each other.

Eighth house: Sex is highlighted; here you may question what you like and don't like in bed. Good idea, but share your thoughts!

Ninth house: Great card for anyone who wants more depth to their philosophy of life. You gravitate to people you can learn from.

Tenth house: You are learning more skills at your job. Put them to good use; they are very valuable for your future.

Eleventh house: You are seen by others as very intelligent and romantic. Great card for finding new friends if used in a card spell.

Twelfth house: Aim high in any intellectual pursuit you are considering; nothing is too farfetched.

Ten of Hearts: Wonderful Rewards.

First house: You are very loved by all who truly know you. Even strangers wish to get closer to you. Go after what you want in life; you won't be disappointed.

Second house: Any earnings will greatly increase at this time. If you want to make any major purchases (such as a car or house), do it. You may make an interesting friend during any business transactions.

Third house: You finally have the time to enjoy yourself. Use it wisely, don't waste it .

Fourth house: Love at home is great; if you want more from your family, just ask.

Fifth house: Buy something fun—a fun toy or that new outfit you always wanted (it will look great on you).

Sixth house: Everything at work seems to be going great; you have self-esteem. Use it.

Seventh house: Everything has been going well for so long you could become a little bored with your relationship. Think of some new ideas on how to strengthen it.

Eighth house: You receive an offer from a powerful person; you have much to gain from this alliance.

Ninth house: Overseas or local travel or exposure to another culture or lifestyle is offered. If you always wanted more from your career or life, pursue your goals.

Tenth house: You have a substantial amount of prestige. This is a good card for teachers; you get your message across.

Eleventh house: A close friend offers to be your mentor; take him or her up on any business ideas you both share.

Twelfth house: Now is the time to aggressively pursue your dreams; you can now easily obtain all that you desire.

Jack of Hearts: A Light-haired, Young Individual.

First house: This might represent you; either you look and act like the jack of hearts or someone close to you meets the description and sees themselves through you.

Second house: Your money is tied up with someone like this, or he or she will be asking you for a loan.

Third house: A friend or relative will contact you about staying in your home; you both would have a good time.

Fourth house: Someone living in your home or a roommate meets this description.

Fifth house: You will go out on the town with a friend who could end up more than that by the end of the night.

Sixth house: A coworker and you work on a project that makes you both closer.

Seventh house: Your lover is a fair-haired person who is youthful; a very strong love.

Eighth house: A hot and turbulent relationship with the jack of hearts. Enjoy.

Ninth house: You could meet on a trip or in school; this card usually means a future relationship.

Tenth house: This is someone who is important to your career; you cannot advance without the help of this person.

Eleventh house: Friends turn into lovers with this card in this house; usually it is an immature love.

Twelfth house: You have someone always on your mind and in your dreams. It is difficult to think of anything else.

Queen of Hearts: A Blond-haired, Blue-eyed Woman.

First house: You are surrounded by love when you walk down the street; people always ask who you are. You receive all kinds of possibilities with people who want to be your lover or pal. Choose wisely.

Second house: A woman has control of your money; you could be spending your savings on this person.

Third house: A close friend and you gossip about yourselves and others. It is a long overdue lunch; you both have deserved to get together for a while.

Fourth house: You have a member in your family who is completely devoted to you. Surrender.

Fifth house: You have a romantic evening with a beautiful person who is the queen of hearts.

Sixth house: You are responsible for and bound by duty to take care of someone who meets this description.

Seventh house: Your dearest partner in life and you are spending some wonderful times together.

Eighth house: You have a relationship with a woman where she is the caregiver and loves you very much; a truly devoted person.

Ninth house: Your ideas and goals match with a special someone. It also could be a teacher who is having a serious romance with a student. It is a relationship where you learn much about yourself.

Tenth house: A partnership that is also career related. You both complement each other in the highest levels and hold each other in the highest regard.

Eleventh house: A friend who supports you through thick and thin. You are so close that whenever you go somewhere without your friend, people ask where she is.

Twelfth house: You have love on your mind, but somehow it eludes you. You could have an enemy who resembles the queen of hearts.

King of Hearts: A Blond-haired, Blue-eyed Man.

First house: You are the king of hearts. If you are a woman, you are powerful and people look up to you. If you are a man, you are admired and popular.

Second house: You love making money and spending it as well; your finances are tied up with another male individual.

Third house: You will meet or know someone like this card; if you ever wanted to record his or her personal history or interview the person, now is the time.

Fourth house: Home is surrounded by love; you have a very good relationship with your spouse.

Fifth house: You and your lover are very close and have much fun, joy, and laughter.

Sixth house: Your work revolves around a boss who is the king of hearts. He thinks you are wonderful and may want more from you after work hours.

Seventh house: You are partners for life and have achieved what many desire in a relationship, but few accomplish. Your love is of the highest nature.

Eighth house: You have friends or lovers in powerful places. You could receive money from an unknown source.

Ninth house: A long trip with your loved one is indicated. You will go to a luxurious and beautiful resort and learn how much you mean to each other.

Tenth house: You and your partner will achieve great long-term goals together and will be able to make a tidy sum of money.

Eleventh house: If you both ever thought of starting a family, now is the time. Also, a good friend could become more.

Twelfth house: You are obsessed with a person who meets this description; they consume your everyday thoughts.

♣ Clubs

Ace of Clubs: Major Transformation.

First house: Your power and drive are amazing. You have energy to complete some very difficult tasks. If you ever wanted to break out of your rut, you can now. Use this card in a card spell to change your life and find new direction. Only for the bold.

Second house: Money ventures are out of control! If you like to gamble, this can be a very stimulating time for you—but it is not the best time to put all your eggs in one basket.

Third house: Ideas are coming faster than you can control them; use this time to record your thoughts and feelings on a tape recorder.

Fourth house: Life at home is a bit hectic; some major changes in your domestic life could occur.

Fifth house: You are not having a lot of fun right now; your nose is to the grindstone. If your friends ask you out, you tell them you are too busy to be bothered.

Sixth house: This is clearly a card of a workaholic. Only people who work all day and most of the evening have this card. Some fatigue is indicated.

Seventh house: Not a great time for relationships; there has been some discontentment for a while.

Eighth house: Difficulties with transactions; you seem to be doing most of the work. Many times, this card shows that others are passing off their work to you. I have seen this card with many clerical workers who have little control over their work.

Ninth house: A new beginning at school shows a long hard climb or an outlook on life that is much more structured and not nearly as flexible as it was in the past.

Tenth house: Whatever you hoped or dreamed in the future, now is the time to head for those goals; you will eventually get what you want out of life. Great for card spells.

Eleventh house: You think you know what you want out of life, but you are not sure how to get it. Believe in your dream. This is a fighting card.

Twelfth house: There is a tendency to overindulge and feel sorry for oneself. You need to use all the energy you have to feel good about yourself.

Two of Clubs: Difficulties with Projects.

First house: Low energy. You care little about your personal appearance and spend little time taking care of yourself.

Second house: Money is low; you seem to make too little to support yourself. Household repairs could cost you.

Third house: Nothing seems to work right; minor annoyances keep trying your patience. Not a great time to get your ideas across.

Fourth house: Housework and family members are more work than usual. Your home seems to take more away than add to your life. This card is frequently seen in people who are changing residences.

Fifth house: You are not going out and having any fun. You have way too much work to do any kind of leisure activity.

Sixth house: You are caught up in the duties of work; you are doing what you dislike most.

Seventh house: Your relationship is nil or it lacks zest; the spark seems to be eroding.

Eighth house: Sex is not the greatest for either of you; try again later. Do not make any moves to a new lover at this time.

Ninth house: Your thinking is shallow and superficial; you need to spend more time listening to others instead of yourself.

Tenth house: Career-wise, everything seems stuck; this is not a good time for job changes.

Eleventh house: Friends are telling you their troubles; some are keeping you from completing your goals. Do not let them.

Twelfth house: You are tired from so much overwork and fatigue; you cannot seem to have a good time no matter what you do; it will pass.

Three of Clubs: Major Responsibility.

First house: You have a worn-out look about you and have little strength in social niceties. Others see you as being in a lousy mood.

Second house: All your money seems to go to every place you do not want it to; you have little control over your finances.

Third house: Others seem to bother you, especially strangers; all their idle chatter drives you up a wall.

Fourth house: Family members are clinging and whiny; you cannot do more for them, but they ask anyway.

Fifth house: Work and pleasure are the same right now. Whatever you want to do involves both; usually it is attending the functions that you do not like.

Sixth house: Work has little reward for you; many people with this card dream of finding another type of work.

Seventh house: Relationships need a lot of work, either with your significant other or business partner; you have to work to repair the damage done.

Eighth house: You have a lot of work to do with another; most of the time it is someone you want to impress.

Ninth house: If you're a student, this is a time of midterms and finals; If you're not, it just feels that way.

Tenth house: Difficulties with short- and long-term goals; best to keep a low profile.

Eleventh house: Friendships take a lot of work; a decision needs to be made if you will continue one special relationship.

Twelfth house: Creativity is at an all-time low; not a great time to act on any new ideas.

Four of Clubs: Little Progress.

First house: The opinions you have of yourself are not completly true; you give the aura of always being right.

Second house: Everything you own you have worked very hard for; sometimes this card reveals someone who is a little selfish.

Third house: You're trying to produce a lot, but right now you're producing little; It is a lot like writer's block.

Fourth house: Life at home is not at all pleasant; you could feel like you are spending too much time at home.

Fifth house: Children or young people could be acting up right now; it is hard to be patient with them.

Sixth house: Your health is a little poor; many people catch colds and the flu when this card shows up. Beware!

Seventh house: You are holding a grudge against someone close to you; let it go. It will hurt you in the long run.

Eighth house: You are spending too much time hoping someone else will come along and make your world better. Ask yourself why.

Ninth house: Not the best time for travel; if you go camping, the weather could be unpleasant.

Tenth house: Chances are you were passed over for a promotion; not a great time for a career boost.

Eleventh house: Stop blaming others for your shortcomings; it hurts your relationships with others.

Twelfth house: Sleepless nights; too much on your mind. Try to let it go.

Five of Clubs: Small Accomplishments.

First house: Others see you as someone who is accomplished; you see yourself in the same manner.

Second house: Investments are growing and you have good insight to increase your wealth.

Third house: You can influence others right now; do not give too much away by idle chatter.

Fourth house: Good time to finish long-term goals around your home; you could make some money from your home.

Fifth house: You are starting to enjoy yourself again but it is difficult not to think of work.

Sixth house: Long-term goals are paying off; you find some joy at work.

Seventh house: Trust is made within a relationship; you kiss and make up.

Eighth house: A title or legal decree looks like it might work out to your favor. It is still too early to claim victory.

Ninth house: Your hopes and desires fit with your goals. You have not always been this realistic.

Tenth house: This is the closest you have been in a long time to achieving a major career goal. Hard work does pay off.

Eleventh house: A friend and you have some farfetched ideas that may work out.

Twelfth house: Convince yourself you can do better; you can and will.

Six of Clubs: Procrastination.

First house: You see yourself as a very busy person who has a lot to do; others see you as a procrastinator and a little lazy. Which one are you?

Second house: Take better care of the possessions you own; many of your belongings show an excess of use.

Third house: You need to spend more time cleaning up and finishing any projects; expect ones involving paper.

Fourth house: Some family members feel that you take advantage of them and impose too much.

Fifth house: Are you too pushy in what you want to do and ignoring what others want to do for fun? It's time to lighten up.

Sixth house: Work is not getting done, although you give the appearance of someone who is overworked.

Seventh house: Not listening to your partner's complaints makes matters worse; try harder.

Eighth house: Time to finish your will and other legal documents you never get around to.

Ninth house: Time to finish all those long-term projects that are very involved; take it one step at a time.

Tenth house: Why don't you start to go after what you really want out of life? What is holding you back?

Eleventh house: Give more energy and time to others, especially old friends; this card indicates a need to give more.

Twelfth house: Mentally, you are holding yourself back from your dreams; be brave.

Seven of Clubs: Reflect on Your Plans.

First house: Physical appearance is very important to you right now and also affects how others see you. You are in a period of examination that can make you look and act different.

Second house: Trying to decide what and where to invest and other major financial questions and purchases are key right now. Usually, this card indicates a dissatisfied customer.

Third house: Thinking is blocked; you are spending too much time on ideas that may or may not work. This is not the best time for reflection.

Fourth house: Family members are telling you the way things should be; listen to your own heart.

Fifth house: Socially, everything doesn't seem to pan out; you are wondering what really interests you.

Sixth house: This card usually means to volunteer; you are spending time trying to decide what's the best way to get involved with your community.

Seventh house: Many "shoulds" are entering your relationships; you question the best way to go and your needs.

Eighth house: Some major decision is coming up that will affect you for a lifetime; you need to keep a clear head.

Ninth house: The course you should take academically as well as a life improvement are prominently focused.

Tenth house: What to do about your career? Should you change or stay on the same path? It is best to wait a while.

Eleventh house: Questioning some of your friendships and how you and your friends relate to each other is important; you may take advantage of some of your associates.

Twelfth house: Opinions of yourself are not in step with who you really are; you are kidding yourself.

Eight of Clubs: Forge Ahead on All Plans.

First house: Energy is low and you drag yourself everywhere or, as my mom used to say, "You look like something the cat dragged in." It is not a pretty sight.

Second house: Financial things seem to be very low. Will you ever make it out of the slump? Keep trying.

Third house: Too many petty details are clouding what you really want to accomplish; you must take control.

Fourth house: Do not spend so much time worrying about your family; when you are so anxious you push them away.

Fifth house: When you are in the company of others, you tend to be a wet blanket.

Sixth house: Your responsibilities at work never seem to end; you are wondering if it is really worth all the effort you put in.

Seventh house: Is your partnership worth all the endless energy you put into it? Only you can predict.

Eighth house: Money is tied up in places that are not that accessible; you need to expand your resources.

Ninth house: A lot of questioning about future goals; you ask yourself if you are on the right track.

Tenth house: Will you ever reach your goals? It seems that the struggle is too long. Keep pushing.

Eleventh house: Hope and inspiration seem to pass you by; this is the time to wait for new ideas to come.

Twelfth house: You are dissatisfied about the state of affairs concerning yourself and others.

Nine of Clubs: Work on Yourself.

First house: This is the time you must get it together and sharpen up your appearance and attitude.

Second house: It has been a long time since you spent your money on yourself; you are now getting ready to change.

Third house: Work out any differences you have in communication; this is not the time to be stubborn.

Fourth house: Home is not where your heart is; you spend too much time starting projects around the home and then you leave them half-finished.

Fifth house: Any social engagement and receiving of others as a host should be started immediately; you owe others.

Sixth house: Finish what you have started; you will drive yourself crazy unless you get your work off your desk.

Seventh house: Work on your relationship or leave; you are now coming to the end of your partnership as you know it.

Eighth house: Not enough sex or other problems with your partner; face up to what will change your life to make it more fulfilling.

Ninth house: Not a great time to travel; many times, this card indicates a transfer to another city.

Tenth house: This is the time to put your nose to the grindstone; do not overlook any details that may later come back to haunt you.

Eleventh house: Do not get involved with anything that can keep you off your path.

Twelfth house: This is not the time to change your dreams and desires; keep to what you know as true.

Ten of Clubs: Major Changes.

First house: You need to get yourself in order. If you have been procrastinating on any event in your life, you could miss some upcoming major opportunity.

Second house: Do what you need to do to finish up any last money transaction; you will need to cash out some resources so it is best to have everything in order.

Third house: Finish all correspondences, send out all overdue thank-you notes, and return all business calls; your relaxed attitude with these matters is starting to bother close associates.

Fourth house: Moving or remodeling is in the cards; this is a good time to finish all projects in the home and smooth out any problems.

Fifth house: Time to pay all social debts; pick up the tab for a function that you have invited others to.

Sixth house: Health issues are here; you need to pay close attention so you do not get into an accident.

Seventh house: Working out long-term solutions right now to you and your partner's relationship is mandatory to keep the fire burning.

Eighth house: This card could mean the end of a lawsuit, a legal problem that all will finally be over, or the end of any kind of document problem.

Ninth house: The end of your efforts is here; if you have pursued a goal with drive, success will be yours.

Tenth house: The day is coming to an end; many of your long-term planning and career goals will finally be completed; success.

Eleventh house: Some of your wilder schemes and unusual ideas just might work; put them to good use.

Twelfth house: It is difficult for you to see yourself as successful; you still cling to the ideas that you are a nobody. It is just not true.

Jack of Clubs: A Brown-haired, Hazel-eyed Individual.

First house: You are the jack of clubs; others see you as a strong, willful person.

Second house: Someone is talking you out of ways to spend your money; remember, it benefits them.

Third house: Work on improving your daily interactions with others; when both of you walk away, you wonder what was really said.

Fourth house: If you are spending more time at home with an individual who fits this description, you are probably getting a lot done around the house.

Fifth house: Nights out on the town with the jack of clubs; a great time to try a new place or go dancing.

Sixth house: Working with the jack of clubs can leave you exhausted during the day; you have a huge amount of responsibility to this person.

Seventh house: This could be your key relationship, either with a child or an adult; it is this person with whom you spend the most time. It is always a demanding relationship.

Eighth house: This is the time you really need to look over the fine print in any document you sign with the jack of clubs.

Ninth house: Travel with the jack of clubs could be more than what you bargain for; you get on each other's nerves.

Tenth house: Goals and long-term career aspirations are tied up with this individual; you must work together to benefit the group and not just each other.

Eleventh house: Spending a lot of free time and work time with the jack of clubs, you both delight in each other's company.

Twelfth house: Dreaming of a person who fits this description, you have an unclear idea of who this person really is.

Queen of Clubs: A Dark-haired, Hazel-eyed Woman.

First house: A very determined person slightly blocks your ideas or goals; they go for what they want and they can be very persuasive. They make great salespersons.

Second house: Any business that involves this type of person would be successful; they have good ideas and lots of energy.

Third house: Small presents and lovely letters could be received from a person of this queen description. Also, if you are an artist, the queen of clubs is your muse.

Fourth house: Someone in your home is the queen of clubs; usually he or she runs the household.

Fifth house: You are spending free time with a very close friend or lover who picks out the spots he or she thinks you should go.

Sixth house: Many times, this is someone you must take care of, such as your mother or another older relative who needs your help.

Seventh house: Your partner is the dominating type; he or she lets their needs be mett at any cost to the relationship.

Eighth house: Giving all that you have is the focus here; someone is asking you to take care of them.

Ninth house: You are trying to attract the attention of a person who means a lot to you; he or she is not sure who you are. Keep trying.

Tenth house: Mentors figure prominently; this is a person you need to help you get your promotion. Tread softly, they are quick to anger.

Eleventh house: A friend you are not quite sure of spends way too much of your time complaining about everything.

Twelfth house: The queen of clubs is an enemy who is after more than you bargained for; watch out.

King of Clubs: A Dark-haired, Hazel-eyed Man.

First house: This character is a strong person who has different ideas and goals. If you want to know what they are thinking, just ask; they do not beat around the bush.

Second house: If your stockbroker or accountant looks like this, expect to make some money. Also you could make a business deal with this person.

Third house: You both click mentally as if you both could see each other's mind; a lot in common, you both love to talk.

Fourth house: A person in your home is really king; they act like they own the whole castle. Keep calm.

Fifth house: You have a lovely dinner companion who knows just what to say and who is who; let this person take you to private parties.

Sixth house: Most of the time, this card represents a person in authority. Here, though, it represents a peer who acts like the boss; do not let the person command you.

Seventh house: Husband or wife, this is your marriage partner who likes to tell you how to run your life.

Eighth house: Money coming from an unfamiliar source; the king of clubs handles the transaction.

Ninth house: Chances are that this is a teacher or someone whose teachings you admire; this is a great time to benefit from their teachings.

Tenth house: Spending time with your boss at work and maybe outside the office offers a chance for more in the relationship if you want it.

Eleventh house: A close friend is advising you what to do with your life and what not to do with your life; listen to that person.

Twelfth house: Listening to what others have told you about what you seem to be about has you confused; a person with the description of the king of clubs should not be trusted.

♦ Diamonds

Ace of Diamonds: Money, Money, and More Money.

First house: Charismatic and lovely, you get a lot of attention from people when you walk down the street. If you want to achieve anything that takes personal risk, do so; this is the time.

Second house: Spending money on your loved one and yourself is very enjoyable; you give and give and give.

Third house: Creating brings you joy, but you are analyzing your art too much; remember to just enjoy it for now.

Fourth house: You love your home, everything is fine, but you are spending less time at home, not more. Think about it.

Fifth house: Seeing flaws in anything social will make it a lot less fun; many times, this card is for people who host large events.

Sixth house: Work is fine, but you just cannot help noticing that you want more; do not be so greedy.

Seventh house: Real and imaginary, you are looking at your partner with much more emphasis on whatever he or she does that affects you.

Eighth house: A chance to expand yourself through your experiences with money via another is highlighted.

Ninth house: What does enjoyment mean? What are the differences between true love and fun? Can one learn to enjoy? You are asking yourself many questions to see if your romantic and monetary notions are real compared to others.

Tenth house: High idealism can leave you in for a shock. Everything from how to make a living to who you think your ideal mate should be is up in the air. You wonder what you will end up with.

Eleventh house: You are spending time with a friend who tests your love and money; is the relationship worth what you think it is?

Twelfth house: Life is good; you have a great outlook on life and are ready to make some major decisions involving great sums of money or a career.

Two of Diamonds: A Turn toward the Better.

First house: Confidence is on the rise; you are feeling better about yourself than you have in a long time.

Second house: Money is improving but the growth is slow; spend it wisely.

Third house: Ideas and conversation are flowing; you are now much more at ease at small talk. You tell good jokes.

Fourth house: Home improvements with your relationships as well as your belongings; you start to take care of what really matters.

Fifth house: Spend more free time on what you care about; this is a good time to start a family or enrich the life of a child.

Sixth house: Responsibilities are much more easy to handle; your new-found confidence seems to get you through anything.

Seventh house: Spend time with a loved one to create something new. If you ever dreamed of working from your home, it is a great time to start a home business.

Eighth house: A surprise—either you or another start a new major project; it could change your life.

Ninth house: Finally others are responding to your thoughts and feelings; you are finding that others do take you seriously at home and work.

Tenth house: This is the start of something big; you are making major plans on how to change your career and this card gives you the opportunity to do just that.

Eleventh house: Intuition is strong; give into any gut feelings you have about others because your perceptions are right.

Twelfth house: You now have extreme clarity about yourself; you can see yourself for whom you really are and you can appreciate your unique gifts.

Three of Diamonds: Desires Come True.

First house: People and places are starting to click; you are at the right place at the right time and it is wise to take advantage of any opportunities.

Second house: You are spending more than you make on whatever catches your eye; this is not the best time to go to expensive and exclusive shops.

Third house: Great time to jot down any creative ideas or thoughts; success in any matters relating to sales.

Fourth house: Stay with family members; more now then ever this is the time when you could really enjoy each other.

Fifth house: You dazzle family and friends, strangers notice you; this is a perfect card for those who are entertainers or wish to impress others.

Sixth house: Striving for perfection in yourself and all that you do can slow you down; you are trying too hard.

Seventh house: Communication flows easily between you and a long-term business partner concerning relevant new ideas.

Eighth house: Good time for sex or to find a new intense friend; you'll both benefit from the relationship.

Ninth house: Time to take a trip; you'll learn much about yourself from conversations with strangers you meet along the way.

Tenth house: The projects you always wanted to try at work are headed your way; you are ready for any major challenges.

Eleventh house: If you ever played around with the idea of inventing a new gadget, you may have an award-winning idea; try it out.

Twelfth house: You're optimistic and have a sunny outlook on life; this will get you far. Some people will ask you what kind of happy drug you are on.

Four of Diamonds: Taking Control.

First house: False security is surrounding you; you have a lot of confidence on the outside, little on the inside. Time for balance and self-examination.

Second house: You have spent more money than you actually have; this card usually appears to someone who overspends on his or her credit card.

Third house: You are not listening to what people are really saying and you should; you are being too self-absorbed at this time.

Fourth house: Creating and developing your lifestyle is the key; you ask yourself what kind of person you really are and what you want to be.

Fifth house: You are proud of your accomplishments and you tell others who you are and what you have done. Others look up to you, but you do not feel their approval.

Sixth house: This is the time when you feel that work is beneath you and some of your chores are too mundane; you look for a change.

Seventh house: Love and/or marriage is going great, but you feel like something is missing.

Eighth house: More responsibility is headed your way, but you do not want it. In fact, you turn your head around to pretend it is not happening.

Ninth house: Ambition and drive make you want to work for what you really want out of life and your stubbornness amazes others.

Tenth house: Career starts are slow and you are impatient; although your goals are closer to being achieved, they are not close enough.

Eleventh house: Expecting way too much of others is wearing thin, even in the closest relationships. You are being too immature and spoiled.

Twelfth house: Everything is going smoothly, but you cannot help but wonder when it is going to backfire.

Five of Diamonds: Go Out on a Limb.

First house: If you ever wanted to impress others, this is the time to do it. Be bold, wear red, and talk loudly; this is not the time to be a wallflower.

Second house: Spend the energy and time to go after what you need to make you monetarily happy; do not take no for an answer.

Third house: Talk can be cheap, but yours is golden. This is a wonderful card for those in sales or advertising. Present pitches and presentations now.

Fourth house: Family is wonderfully supportive of you and this is a good time to have them back you up on any new ideas or projects.

Fifth house: This is a great time to cash in on any creative thought. This time, your creations could take hold in the world.

Sixth house: Your health is very good; this is the best you've felt in years. It is also a good time to start new diets or exercise programs.

Seventh house: Meeting the people you need to meet is very important; do not be shy with a stranger.

Eighth house: If you ever wanted to sue or fight for what you want, this card is on your side; you'll have success.

Ninth house: Great time for some major changes. Be aggressive in whatever you decide to do.

Tenth house: Finally you have figured out what is missing in your life and you are going for it; look out, world, here you come!

Eleventh house: Inspiration and wisdom are with you; turn your flashes of insight into what you want.

Twelfth house: The dreams you have long kept to yourself are about to unfold, everything will work out fine.

Six of Diamonds: Creativity at an All-Time High.

First house: Much energy is needed to substantiate what you have already accomplished. Some people who have received this card in a reading have said that they are just worn out but do not have the time to take it easy.

Second house: Others see you as a human whirlwind and this is the time to tackle any major household projects.

Third house: Others need you and are asking for your support in ways you never thought possible. Some are more talk than action.

Fourth house: Great time to work on that home business you always dreamed of starting; go, go, go! It could be very successful.

Fifth house: Business and pleasure mix very well right now; this is a card for those with an expense account. Now is the time to treat yourself well and to treat others well also.

Sixth house: If you like working overtime or moonlighting, it is a favorable time. This is the card you need to be successful. Use it in a card spell.

Seventh house: Love and money go together like bees and honey; this is a great time to form a real partnership in many ways.

Eighth house: Make plans for your retirement today; start thinking long-term of what you want to have in life. Anything that you start now in terms of investment will be successful in a while.

Ninth house: A lot of action right now, lots of drive. It is a great time to take a business trip.

Tenth house: You are meeting the right people and are starting to get introduced into the social circle that you have always dreamed; have a good time and do not forget to network.

Eleventh house: If you ever wanted children, now is a good time to start; but be careful if you do not want any. You can also use this time to birth creative ideas instead of making babies.

Twelfth house: You are filled with easy-going, pleasant, and happy thoughts; this is a card that indicates an optimist.

Seven of Diamonds: A New Look.

First house: The first house is the actual drive it takes to change what you want about yourself. Some people with this card are contemplating cosmetic surgery.

Second house: Time to move to either a new neighborhood or a new city; you are looking for an alternative lifestyle.

Third house: This is the time to set some people straight; you tell others what you really think and you hold firm to your principles.

Fourth house: If you ever wanted to change your home, now is the time; you may desire a new home altogether.

Fifth house: Trying a different kind of entertainment is a good idea; seek out the kind of club you have never dared to go to before. Something very interesting is about to happen.

Sixth house: Make your voice be heard; speak out to protest any social injustices; demand that others know what you feel is right.

Seventh house: Great time for you and your love; you are both communicating. You find each other very attractive. For those looking for a mate, the time is near.

Eighth house: Hot, hot sex; but if you do not want to do that, there is at least much passion in everything you do.

Ninth house: Great time to make a major move, such as living in another state or another country. You could meet others who are foreign.

Tenth house: You come across as someone who is powerful or someone to be reckoned with; go for what you are after, do not hold back.

Eleventh house: You have some pretty wild ideas about what is real and what is not. Take advantage of this creativity; you can go far with it now.

Twelfth house: Be daring; do what you want. You have never told others what you really want, do it now. The sky is the limit, or should I say outer space?

Eight of Diamonds: Any Dream Is Possible.

First house: You are making the key decisions right now; in short, you call the shots with anything you take on. This is a very powerful card.

Second house: If you want to wheel and deal, this is a good time for stocks and bonds and also for making some quick cash.

Third house: This is the time to finally organize your ideas for the great American novel or another literary project. You really can write.

Fourth house: Your family is first and they are very cooperative. If you have any family members with money or jewels, you could successfully ask them for them.

Fifth house: This is a great card for anyone who has tried to live off their art. You can finally cash in on your creativity or sell creative ideas; the right people are near you.

Sixth house: Getting what you want from work, health, and spirituality is in the cards—do not hold back, ask for what you desire.

Seventh house: If you are trying to make a decision about a marriage or a partnership, this is the time that you start to make some real decisions.

Eighth house: An offer to invest in either yourself or another is here; it indicates making some hard choices in life about what your needs really are.

Ninth house: You can influence others to agree with you in anything you suggest; this card also indicates a journey.

Tenth house: A great card for publishers, writers, or musicians. You can get the green light for any long-term projects. Even those who are not involved in any creative endeavor will achieve some success; you certainly have some great ideas now.

Eleventh house: You have loving and adoring friends who can help you in the world of business. It is also a good time to solicit others for business.

Twelfth house: You now have the courage to face your fears; you can conquer anything if you try.

Nine of Diamonds: Expansion in Earthly Goods.

First house: You're expecting everything to come your way and that you deserve the best; a definite card for those who hold their head high.

Second house: You are secure in your finances and wages; you always know how much you have. If you want to expand your resources, do so now.

Third house: This is a great time to become computer literate, if you are not so already. If you do use a computer, it is time to upgrade your system.

Fourth house: Look around for a real estate deal; it could be a time to make some real money. This card also indicates a comfortable, steady family life.

Fifth house: Splurge and buy those concert tickets you really want or go to that restaurant you have been longing to try. Whatever you like to do for fun you need to do with total abandonment.

Sixth house: Try a new sport, the more invigorating the better; do not hold back for any reason.

Seventh house: You need to get some issues off your chest so be vocal and tell your partner your needs; they will respond.

Eighth house: Help an old relative get rid of their old belongings; you can find many treasures. It benefits both of you.

Ninth house: Time to finish up all those old projects; you need to set your sights higher and not hold yourself back.

Tenth house: Do not procrastinate on any long-term goals, especially if you have been wavering on issues and ideas. Do not stop yourself from completing your goals; there is no longer any reason to delay.

Eleventh house: Act on your intuition and let it guide you to what you need, but beware of daydreaming. This is a terrible time for those who have their heads in the sand; they will miss opportunities.

Twelfth house: You're looking through rose-colored glasses—everything is going so well, why would it change? Do not miss any chances because of a slack attitude; you are not on a permanent vacation.

Ten of Diamonds: Great Fortune, Great Luck.

First house: Because you are charismatic and strong, others ask you about your ancestor line. Are you of royal blood or of some strong descendant from a noble tribe? You command others.

Second house: Forge ahead with business ideas. You deserve the best in life. What you project is what you will receive.

Third house: Spending time on a short weekend getaway does a lot for you; it is possible to locate that dream vacation spot you have always desired.

Fourth house: You are into gourmet cooking in the house and others admire your culinary skills and your beautiful home. You feel close to your family. When I find this card in a reading—no matter who I am reading for—the person smiles in peace and contentment when I mention their home.

Fifth house: This is a great time to network at parties, either ones that you throw or ones you are invited to. Everyone notices that this is not the time to be shy; it is the time to make contacts to further yourself.

Sixth house: Others ask you to be involved in a major project at work or to volunteer in your community. This is an opportunity for growth.

Seventh house: Any ideas that involve risk (outside of risk to you and your loved ones) are favorable; this is a great time for business risks.

Eighth house: You have much power and strength for getting things done. This is a great energizing card. Others ask you how you accomplish so much.

Ninth house: Whenever this card comes into a reading in this house, I always suggest one thing: the person needs to go back to school either to take a course or go after a degree. This is a wonderful education card, although some people benefit by learning through travel or doing. This is not a card to take lightly—action is mandatory no matter what direction you decide to take.

Tenth house: Wow! This is the card you want if you are making any type of career moves or long-term planning. You can absolutely change your life for the better. If you snooze you may lose, so go for it.

Eleventh house: Making the connections you need is happening easier now than ever; you are on the right track to doing what you really love in life. Enjoy.

Twelfth house: Spending time alone to plot out what you need in life is making everything go easier for you, but do not slow down; this is the time to pursue your dreams.

Jack of Diamonds:

Brown-haired, Green-eyed Young Individual.

First house: The jack of diamonds represents you. Always on the move, with plenty of ideas and goals, you can charm anyone. You are known as a person who can get the job done; this is a great card for a self-starter.

Second house: Probably you are working on some type of business venture that could be a career risk. You can be reckless with money at this time.

Third house: A relative will be calling on you soon; both of you have much to catch up on and you will reminisce about the good old days. You should definitely catch up on any correspondence that you have neglected in the past.

Fourth house: Usually this is a house guest who changes all the rules in your home; but it can also be anybody who disturbs the peace, including neighbors.

Fifth house: A persistent person will want to drag you along to some intimate social functions. Go along, do not be such a stick in the mud. What do you have to lose?

Sixth house: Lots of energy and drive. This is a great time to try a dangerous sport with a pro such as the jack of diamonds. This person will help you to find out your physical limitations.

Seventh house: A partner or close friend who keeps you going and keeps you young will change your relationship; there could be some rebellion on both sides.

Eighth house: This card will inspire you to reach out to others whom you have ignored in the past; do not hold back.

Ninth house: This person is challenging your values and ideas of philosophy; it is a rare opportunity to see life from a totally different viewpoint. If you like a challenge, invite your friend along; you are both in for a roller-coaster ride.

Tenth house: You are not easily swayed from the path that you are on. Not many detours for you. Your hard work will soon pay off.

Eleventh house: This is probably a rebellious child in your life or one who is ready to take on the world. From a toddler to an adult, this person is testing to see how he or she will fit in the outside world.

Twelfth house: A determined mind-set. Now is the time to plot what action you want to take to go after your dreams. This card also indicates jealousy. Watch what you say about others.

Queen of Diamonds:

A Brown-haired, Green-eyed Woman.

First house: You are the queen of diamonds or you are acting the part; you command quite an appearance. Seldom are you overlooked in a crowded room. Others look up to you and desire to be near you. Be choosy and pick only those who are worthy.

Second house: Your money is tied up with someone who is the queen of diamonds. This could mean you are paying off debts to this person, such as alimony or child support.

Third house: Great ideas and collaborations with another. Right now you are both more talk than do; this is because you are tossing around new ideas.

Fourth house: You could be sharing your living space with another individual who likes to control the decorating and the menu. For those who desire a glamorous homemaker, this is normally a wonderful card to use in a spell.

Fifth house: You both enjoy the same recreational activities. Many people who get this card in a reading enjoy sharing the fine art of living with another.

Sixth house: This is your boss or someone you want to impress. You go to any lengths to meet this person's approval. Ask yourself why.

Seventh house: Your partner and you are very close; you both spend a lot of time together—so much in fact that you each feel naked without the other.

Eighth house: This is someone with whom you have an intense physical relationship or someone whom you desire a great deal. A wise person acts on this basic animal instinct, with permission, of course.

Ninth house: A major lesson comes into play here: just when you thought you knew everything about life, someone comes in and throws you a curve ball.

Tenth house: Lots of drive and energy will help you reach the top; but nobody makes it alone. A person who meets this description is going to help you.

Eleventh house: A friend or relative that you are very close with has some outlandish ideas; your first thought is that they are really crazy—or is it just you?

Twelfth house: You have the unreal expectations of someone to fulfill; what you have lacking may be a problem. Do not put so much responsibility on others.

King of Diamonds: A Brown-haired, Blue-eyed Man.

First house: This card represents you. Others see you as a happy-go-lucky, interesting person. People enjoy you. Make the most of this favorable attitude you project.

Second house: Money and properties are tied up with a person who fits this description. I would suggest that if your stockbroker or money manager does not fit this description, find someone who does. He or she will help you make money.

Third house: Good communication with those you want to reach. Great time to drum up any support you need to achieve long-term goals.

Fourth house: A person who fits this description rules the roost; it is probably this person's home where you dwell. This person is like a landlord or someone who has a strong personality and dominates those who live in the home.

Fifth house: Spend time in a romantic encounter with a special person. Make the most of it and do not worry about how he or she likes to do everything their way.

Sixth house: Collaborate with a person who is the king of diamonds, but do not butt heads; you will lose.

Seventh house: This indicates a close relationship with someone you admire and respect; someone who thinks you are wonderful, too. Enjoy each other and invest in the relationship.

Eighth house: Sexual encounters with a very strong, domineering type. Do you give in?

Ninth house: You could meet this person on a trip, but usually this is someone who teaches you a lesson about life that you will never forget. Be brave.

Tenth house: This is probably your boss or whomever holds the meal ticket over you. Working together makes an interesting challenge; you both benefit greatly.

Eleventh house: This is a good friend who helps you a great deal; this friend loves you very much and will protect you at any cost—much like a big brother type of relationship.

Twelfth house: You are dreaming that you will meet someone, fall in love, and live happily ever after. Is this really the person of your dreams? Yes, dreams really do come true.

♠ Spades

Ace of Spades: Death or Completion.

First house: A major decision confronts you and it will have long-lasting effects. If you choose the right path, destiny will be yours. This is a card that loathes self-pity; hold your head high no matter what others say about you. A time of rebirth can be a positive experience.

Second house: Look carefully over any legal documents that surround you, such as home insurance. Know what is between the lines. It is a bad time to start any new debts.

Third house: Problems with some family members with whom you do not have much contact pop up again. This is the time to, once and for all, finish all issues.

Fourth house: Moving or are you just on the verge of relocating? There are many other issues here besides just a move. Your lifestyle at home is ready for a change. I have also seen this card in readings with people who have many old issues that need to be resolved. Many times, people with this card were abused in their home.

Fifth house: You are not having a lot of fun; either you stay home watching too much TV or you are going to the type of social functions you hate.

Sixth house: Either you have a dead-end job or you are chronically unemployed or underemployed and your health is suffering from it. Start today researching what you really want to do with your life. Do not hold back.

Seventh house: You are seriously examining any major relationship you are in. You have much insight about what is wrong, what needs to be done, and how to fix it. Do not hold back any truth you see with a partner; be loud and complain.

Eighth house: You could gain some money from a will or some family heirlooms; make sure your affairs are in order.

Ninth house: Some of the pleasures you have enjoyed in life are at odds with what you are doing; you need to decide what you really like doing.

Tenth house: This card indicates some confusion about your career. I have seen this card more often than not appear for someone who is about to change careers. The change is not an easy one and there can be many bumps in the road. If you use this card wisely, you can achieve fame in your work.

Eleventh house: You need to be more honest with others and more vocal about what is really going on with you and how you see them. I have also seen this card appear in a reading for people who are either battered wives or verbally abused. You have had enough of being treated unfairly; and unless the jerk who has been bothering you stops it, you'll say good-bye.

Twelfth house: You have been thinking dark thoughts for some time; many people are depressed when this card shows in a reading. How are you feeling (really)? If you have feelings of distress, you need to vent them.

You may want to talk more in-depth with a counselor if this card appears.

Two of Spades: Wistfulness.

First house: Look out for any minor accidents, such as tripping or falling; this is a bad time to do any outdoor sports. Best to keep a clear head and not take any unnecessary risks.

Second house: The grass looks greener on the other side; a tendency to want to keep up with the Joneses no matter how unrealistic that is at this time. Do not worry about what you do not have, concentrate on what you do have.

Third house: Do not make any major arrangements such as travel plans or social plans. Communication gets confused and you could make some errors in planning.

Fourth house: Harboring some resentment toward a family member gets you nowhere; examine your feelings. Do not speak out in anger.

Fifth house: Nothing interests you. Now you find it hard to do anything that was once pleasurable. It is like looking at a newspaper to find a weekend activity and not finding anything interesting to do.

Sixth house: Usually this card comes into play for someone who is not feeling well or could stand to lose some weight. You need a better approach to health.

Seventh house: Low energy in your love life; not a lot of pep. Take time to slow down and reconnect with one another. Also, this can be an dissatisfied bachelor or bachelorette card.

Eighth house: Not a lot of trust right now in others; a little bit of paranoia surrounds you. How much you let it run your life is up to you.

Ninth house: Some plans involving others do not work out the way you want them to. This card usually indicates that others are trying to boss you around; do not allow it.

Tenth house: Everything is taking much longer than you had planned. Details keep changing from moment to moment; do not lose sight of your main goals.

Eleventh house: A friend is not as helpful as they have been in the past or as they present themselves. Do not count on others so much.

Twelfth house: You are unclear on what you think and feel at this time. Do not worry so much; everything will change.

Three of Spades: Superficiality or Stubbornness.

First house: You see yourself as a beautiful, fun, interesting person; others do not. You need to stop kidding yourself about your persona and work on not coming across so strong.

Second house: Are your finances way out of control? Do you think life or the government owes you a living? Well, it doesn't. You and only you are responsible for your debts and finances.

Third house: Ideas and thoughts are very shallow; you need to work on how you express yourself. Others do not listen to your mindless jabber.

Fourth house: Unrealistic expectations about your home and family will cause major problems in the future. Look at this situation very carefully.

Fifth house: Problems with children or small pets? You need help with them right now. Courage and self-help books will steer you in the right direction.

Sixth house: What exactly do you want from your job? Does it seem to be a dead end? You would benefit yourself as well as others if you volunteered to work with others who need your skills; you have much to offer.

Seventh house: Look at how you relate to others. Are you compassionate to and interested in your significant other, or do you want to throw in the towel and call it quits? Self-discovery awaits you.

Eighth house: The demands you are receiving from others are making you resentful; some days you feel overwhelmed with all that is asked of you.

Ninth house: This is a great time for self-discovery and expression. Listen to what others say and do. If you are narrow-minded concerning any subject, it will be channeled in an unusual way.

Tenth house: You have unclear goals or some unusual ideas of what you can do in life. You need to take a long, hard look at what you are truly capable of doing. When I see this card come up in a reading, the person always tells me that he or she is as gifted as someone who is famous in a certain field. For example, they say, "I could be as good a painter as Picasso even though I have never painted." Not only do they sound stupid, but they look like a jerk to others. Watch what you say about yourself with this card.

Eleventh house: Evaluate how you behave with your friends. Do you reluctantly go with the crowd or are you independent in thoughts and feelings? You probably spend too much time trying to conform.

Twelfth house: Life seems to be treating you unkindly. Everything you want goes effortlessly for others, so why are so many things difficult for you? Do not walk around with the "why me" syndrome; nobody likes a crybaby. Hold your head high; you will gain more respect.

Four of Spades: Difficult Beginnings.

First house: You have been working a long time to improve yourself and wondering if it will do any good. It will and you are on your way to success.

Second house: Long-term planning is something you have been avoiding. I see this card a lot around tax time. I tell people the same story: make an appointment with a financial counselor; it is never too late to plan.

Third house: A relative who has angered you in the past will resurface again. You need to decide how to take control of the situation and make some hard decisions about the relationship. Do not whimp out; confront them on their past behavior.

Fourth house: Many past issues, especially with your mother, are surfacing. Her voice is reaching you in everything you do. Are you going to be haunted by past issues or will you embrace and deal with them? It is your choice.

Fifth house: Ghoulishness delights; you are interested in the macabre and spending your free time in ghostly pursuits. Happy haunting.

Sixth house: Take it easy; an old injury could resurface. Your body is warning you to slack off; do not ignore it.

Seventh house: Your partner and you are growing apart. It would be wise to use this warning to patch up any potential problems so that things do not get out of hand.

Eighth house: Criticism about yourself and others can destroy your self-esteem; do not take everything so hard.

Ninth house: This is a wonderful time of self-examination. Why do you do the things you do? Look long term, do not be shortsighted.

Tenth house: No time for a career change. Many times, this card shows up when office politics are heating up.

Eleventh house: Friends are a little glum; you all are a little bored. Will they ever stop their whining?

Twelfth house: Many ideas and plans are floating through your mind; how will you put them all together? It is a bit chaotic. A good time to sort through your thoughts.

Five of Spades: Depression or Major Obstacles.

First house: You are stopping yourself from getting what you know you need from life; you are frequently your own worst enemy.

Second house: You have a smaller bank account than you tell others you have; be honest with yourself about your finances.

Third house: You are at odds with a family member; you both need to be more flexible.

Fourth house: This is not a great time for changes in the home; keep everything the same if possible.

Fifth house: Either you stay home too much or, when you do go out, you do not enjoy what you are doing.

Sixth house: Some old injury could pop up again; do not work out too hard. This card appears when you could do something very serious such as put your back out.

Seventh house: You are harboring old resentments about a relationship, but you can use this time to free yourself, to break with the past. It is best not to go to bed mad.

Eighth house: Not much interest in sex or opening yourself up to others. This is a good time to reflect.

Ninth house: What do you really want out of life? What makes you happy? You need to make some hard decision on what risks you need to take to achieve your goals.

Tenth house: Work seems the same day after day; tap into your daydreams and let your imagination run wild.

Eleventh house: Friends and offspring can bring much disappointment right now; do not put too much stock in others' opinions.

Twelfth house: Depression is with you. Do not take this card lightly; find someone you can talk to.

Six of Spades: Courage and a Strong Will.

First house: Frequently this card shows up in a reading for people who have put aside what they want in life to benefit others. It is a duty card and, although you may not have asked for the responsibility, it was forced upon you. It is up to you to handle the job properly and give in gracefully when needed—or to fight back if necessary.

Second house: You may need to fight for what is rightfully yours; do not let what you want slip by. Bite the bullet and kick butt.

Third house: Others frequently misunderstand you. It is up to you to explain yourself better and not to expect others to know your desires.

Fourth house: Many times, this card indicates the black sheep phenomenon. If you feel unaccepted by your family, you must learn to stick up for yourself and tell others your side of the story.

Fifth house: You are feeling resentful because you are not telling others what you enjoy and so you are letting them pick out your leisure activities; this is your problem. If you want to see a different kind of movie than they do, speak up. What do you have to lose?

Sixth house: Your work is not for you. Look at your strengths and consider applying for a new job; you do not have to be stuck.

Seventh house: Communicate with your partner. Do not stay mad. Find what you had in common in the first place. This card usually indicates that you are the caregiver in the relationship.

Eighth house: Do not let a lawyer or another fight your battles and then think everything will be taken care of. You need to take charge yourself; clarity is the key here.

Ninth house: Your hopes and aspirations do not necessarily fit in with your reality. Decide what you want and do not get off the path.

Tenth house: Others at work take advantage of you. You are doing more than your fair share of the workload. Speak out; do not be timid now.

Eleventh house: Your friends take more than they give. They feel great, but you do not. Demand more balance in the relationship.

Twelfth house: You are blocking yourself away from your creativity. What are you going to do about it? Stop procrastinating.

Seven of Spades: Taking Risks.

First house: This is the time to gear up and get some perspective on who you are and what you want out of life.

Second house: Money obstacles have held you back from pursuing some of your interests; you now have a chance to look at what you have instead of what you do not have.

Third house: Time to use ideas that you have not used in the past; this is a great card for the artistic blocks that have held you back.

Fourth house: Do not let your family tell you who you are. This is for people who are so heavily programmed by their family that they are paralyzed. They are overwhelmed by so much in their life that it is holding them back from reaching their potential.

Fifth house: You need to push yourself in taking better care of yourself. This card shows up for people who are poor groomers. They like wearing clothes that do not fit or they need an updated hairstyle.

Sixth house: It is a great time to encourage better eating habits and posture.

You are projecting an image that is less than popular; you can control your eating habits much better.

Seventh house: Do not let your partner take so much control over you; stick up for yourself and have more say in the relationship.

Eighth house: Someone is holding out on you and is being less than honest; find out. You cannot change others, but you can change yourself.

Ninth house: You need to put a plan in action to achieve your dreams; nothing will happen unless you start to act.

Tenth house: The career you wanted is not available or is hard to reach. If the type of work you want is different than what you are doing, start to work on job search goals.

Eleventh house: Friends and children could be a bit unreachable right now; you need to put this in perspective and set limits with them.

Twelfth house: The subconscious is a remarkable tool; use it to input affirmations and eradicate negative thoughts.

Eight of Spades: Immediate Change.

First house: Feeling a little out of control, that you are predestined to live your reality? You can change how you look at yourself and this will affect how others see you.

Second house: You have been stuck in indecision for so long that the feeling of being overwhelmed is running your life. Being stuck in a pool of murk is wearing you thin. Frequently when this card comes up in a reading, the person says to me, "How much longer will it last?" The answer is almost always the same: it is up to you.

Third house: Start to find your voice; speak out and articulate for those that are not being heard. Get on your soapbox and speak your mind; great card for political activists.

Fourth house: Who is the adult in your family? Are you the responsible one or are you the adolescent that cannot seem to grow up? Break the ties that bind you and have the courage to look hard at yourself and how you fit in with the family.

Fifth house: More work than fun; this is the card of the couch potato. Only you can change the habits of what you do and do not do for entertainment.

Sixth house: You are feeling dissatisfied with your life work and not sure what you should be doing. When this card comes up in a reading, advise the person to see a career counselor.

Seventh house: More maturity is needed in your primary relationship; you need to either go with the flow or change course. Your partner will not be motivated to change until you try a different path.

Eighth house: Your partner is not very supportive of your dreams or aspirations; it is difficult to accomplish something without recognition. This is an area of life where you need to work it out by yourself; you will receive more self-respect if you do.

Ninth house: Difficulties in any examination. This card almost always shows up in readings when a student has a major test he or she has not studied for.

Tenth house: Many times, people feel that this is a time when life has passed them over and they are stuck with doing the same old thing over and over again. Remember, you can change old patterns!

Eleventh house: A friend that you have known for a long time no longer seems like old friend. You are both wearing on each other's nerves; it is time to take a break from each other.

Twelfth house: Not a great time to overindulge. This is an excessive card and frequently seen as a card that indicates way too much of a good thing. Once when I was giving a reading, this card showed up—and when the person sat down she was so drunk she fell off her stool. Enough said.

Nine of Spades: Radical Difference.

First house: Do not cut off your nose to spite your face. If your loved ones are calling you unreasonable, ask yourself why. Do not act as if the way you are is everyone else's problem. It is not.

Second house: What do you want long term? Many times, this is the card of someone deeply in debt or someone who makes very little money. Make a move to change this situation.

Third house: Do not make much out of nothing; gossip can hurt you. Some will misunderstand what you are saying; it is better to be quiet.

Fourth house: It is better to get some clear space from your family and your home; watch out for accidents at home.

Fifth house: Develop a more flexible attitude, especially with the younger people in your life. You do not have to be so rigid; others will label you nice but no fun.

Sixth house: You are feeling dissatisfaction with your body and your general health. Some experience a vague recurring health problem; seek a second opinion.

Seventh house: Get out of your relationship rut; this is the time to go out and rekindle old romantic interest. A change is long overdue.

Eighth house: Do not start anything new, especially when it involves a new contract. If this is the case and you must sign something, read the fine print carefully.

Ninth house: Try to develop a new, positive attitude. Do not be so worried; it is not going to bring you anything.

Tenth house: Dark times around your business. Not the best time to make many changes, but be open to new ideas and others will help you.

Eleventh house: When this card shows up, it almost always indicates that the person is working overtime with an overdemanding person. Make time to help yourself more than helping others.

Twelfth house: Waiting around for everything to happen may involve a very long (endless?) wait.

Ten of Spades: Achievement Over Obstacles.

First house: Transformation of your whole image is here. This transformation is beyond a new hairstyle or coloring your hair; it is a change from within. Others who have not seen you for a long time do not recognize you. One of my clients was a handsome, successful stockbroker. I was surprised to find this card in his first house. When I told him that he had just transformed and was now adjusting to this major change, he replied that this was true. He said he used to be obese. In fact, he was grossly overweight most of his life. Now he was starting to address the fact that not only was he very rich, but he was also extremely handsome. With that combination, he probably will not be single for very much longer.

Second house: No longer being strapped for resources or finally making that last payment on a loan puts money in a whole different perspective. More than ever, you understand money's true power and meaning.

Third house: Recently you have learned a harsh lesson in this game called life. Congratulations, you are now thinking in a completely different way.

Fourth house: You are breaking away from your family. Often it is a rite of passage; maybe a first home, marriage, or a new baby. This is a very strong card and how it signifies home change is intense. In California after a major earthquake, many victims had this card in this house; their homes were changed forever.

Fifth house: Starting to explore unseen territory will benefit you. You begin to venture out on some new avenues of entertainment, such as visiting nightclubs you have never dared to go to before.

Sixth house: Gaining strength with your health. Many find it a great time to get a new pet. Also, you are finally getting rid of an overdue responsibility you have been carrying around.

Seventh house: Marriage or business relationships could end. Things cannot go the same as they have in the past; there have been too many problems for too long. Something has got to give.

Eighth house: This symbolizes the inheritance of an unpleasant matter and finishing up long-overdue projects. Keep track of records; the IRS may have its eye on you.

Ninth house: You are about to take a leap into the unknown and learn something new. Anything you decide to learn about—especially in the realms of religion, psychology, or philosophy—will change your life for the better.

Tenth house: It is a great time to say, "Take this job and shove it." This card usually comes up for people who hate their jobs and are ready to quit.

Eleventh house: Long-term goals that you have shared with others just did not work out. You are experiencing new ideas and wondering how to implement them. Your answer is just around the corner; dream big and act.

Twelfth house: Sadness has held you back for so long, but you are now thinking of how to end it and no longer cry yourself to sleep. You start to take the long steps of self-empowerment after living in the doldrums for so long; life starts to look good.

Jack of Spades:

A Dark-haired, Dark-eyed Young Individual.

First house: There is much action and you are getting what you want out of life, although you can be your own worst enemy. Sometimes you sabotage yourself and push yourself away from your immediate goals.

Second house: You are spending money too foolishly and giving it away to others who have not earned it.

Third house: Others can misinterpret what you are saying, do not let them convince you that you said something you really did not.

Fourth house: In your home, someone is taking up too much space. I have seen this card come up in many readings; typically my clients refer to these jacks as the roommates from hell.

Fifth house: No matter what your age, if this card shows up, you (or someone close) tend to be a bit of a juvenile delinquent. When you go out on the town, you have moments of being very bad in a good kind of way. This is a great card for theatrical people.

Sixth house: You have many responsibilities with someone who does not appreciate your efforts; many times it is an immature boss.

Seventh house: You and a certain someone spend a lot of hard work trying to help each other in a close relationship. Try to spend more time together; it should help in the long run.

Eighth house: Good time to help others who are not as well off as you; spend time or money on your favorite causes.

Ninth house: You can get caught up in the seedier side of life. This is the card of gamblers; do not risk too much money.

Tenth house: Someone else may beat you out of the promotion at work. Do not be a sore loser; try harder to win next time.

Eleventh house: You are letting a friend boss you around and you tend to try to please them. Long term, this will drive you crazy; say no once in a while.

Twelfth house: You are letting another individual get the best of you; do not let people into your space whom you do not want there.

Queen of Spades: A Dark-haired, Dark-eyed Woman.

First house: A positive self-image does much to help you feel strong and self-assured; you radiate much energy and are in control of your destiny.

Second house: Being a little too generous with a person who meets this description can cause you many problems. Do not give until it hurts; it causes you major hassles in the long run.

Third house: Do not reveal too much about your feelings and how you want your problems to work out; the queen does not have time to listen.

Fourth house: Mother or mother-in-law problems have you all tied up now. I have seen this card surface with people who have to resolve major issues with their mother. Also, you can be called on to help someone who is sick in the family.

Fifth house: Let the queen of spades take you out for a night on the town; it definitely will not be boring.

Sixth house: You do a lot of work with this woman or you must take care of some older person; this is definitely a time that tries your patience.

Seventh house: This is a relationship that is difficult for you both; try to develop a sense of humor about your life.

Eighth house: Work out any subtle or not-so-subtle differences you have with an individual who meets this description; it will do you both a lot of good.

Ninth house: Taking a trip with the queen of spades is a very good idea; you will both learn a lot.

Tenth house: Try to improve yourself at work and gain the support of the office wise woman. The queen of spades will benefit you in the long run.

Eleventh house: More of a foe than a friend, this person has more interest in themselves and their world than in you. Ask yourself the question: what will this card gain from me and what will I lose?

Twelfth house: A lot of negative influence right now; you can easily be persuaded to overindulge and hurt yourself consuming rich food, alcohol, and drugs.

King of Spades: A Dark-haired, Dark-eyed Man.

First house: Strength is with you; this is an opportunity to push yourself and achieve long overdue desires. It is undesirable at this time to feel sorry for yourself. Do not waste your time on what might have been.

Second house: You share your money with someone; you probably have little to say in how it is spent as well.

Third house: You need to get tough and straighten someone out who is not listening to you—which is very difficult. Nothing will happen, however, until it is done.

Fourth house: Someone in your home meets this description or will be visiting you soon. Usually it is a father or a husband. No matter what form they take, they are extremely overbearing.

Fifth house: Going out with a king could get you the best seats in the house or the best table in a restaurant; this person knows everybody.

Sixth house: You have much responsibility. This card usually signifies a boss who lays on the deadlines thick and heavy and you never stand up to the imposition; try to.

Seventh house: Your mate makes most of the important decisions in your relationship, many times without consulting you. You find out second hand about some important matters. What will you do?

Eighth house: There could be a legal dispute going on. This is a person who feels very strongly about issues; a good person to have on your side.

Ninth house: This is probably a teacher or mentor who is in your life now; you could learn a lot from this individual so be open-minded.

Tenth house: Now is a great time to make use of a possible promotion at work. Make strides. Striking out on your own is not a bad idea, either.

Eleventh house: A good friend who will do much for you is around. This person has a short fuse, so do not take him or her lightly. Speak up if this person is unsupportive and you will get results.

Twelfth house: Someone is spreading rumors about you. Do not let others dictate your reality; fight back. Take control of your life!

CHAPTER 6

Sample Readings Using The Wheel of Life Spread

Sample Reading: Tess

Tess is a successful business woman with many friends. She owns and runs Stargazers, a popular metaphysical store, and has others who depend on her to feel good when they purchase something. She is also a counselor. She always asks how people are; she can tune right into people. This was her card reading.

Sophia: This card reading is good for the next couple of weeks—unless it's a trend and then the same cards will show up in another reading. It's only going to show how life is unfolding now and not the long-term future. Okay?

Tess: Yes.

Sophia, shuffling the cards: If you have any issues at this time, it's the time to look at them. They are very immediate. I'll put the cards in three separate piles. Please put them in one pile. Now I'll lay the cards out in a circle, the Zodiac circle.

Tess: Do I need to ask a question or anything?

Sophia: No, the cards will direct the questions. You have the six of spades in the first house, which means that you have a lot of responsibility. Everything personal has been kind of hard. It's like the five of spades where everything is difficult; but with the six you're getting over it.

Tess: Yes, that is true.

Sophia: The queen of spades is in the second house. Your money is tied up with another person, or your home or other issues concern somebody.

Tess: Say more.

Sophia: The queen of spades is a brunette, or if the person is not a brunette he or she has a very dark personality.

Tess: This is the money house?

Sophia: Yes, so it shows your money is tied up; it could be a stockbroker or someone who helps you with your finances. When a card like this shows up, you have a lot of mistrust toward this person. You're looking at this person and wondering if you should put so much faith in him or her. Also, this person can be difficult to deal with. Usually with a queen in the second house there are questions about where resources will go. What am I going to put my money into? How am I going to work things out? It's not a card that means that money is going to come to you. It's more of an evaluation of finances; this is how I want to do something. Interesting, it's a queen, which is a feminine energy, surrounding your money. Does this make sense to you ?

Tess: Yes.

Sophia: Okay. So that is what is going on with the queen of spades. Your third house has the four of diamonds. Now is the time to do something if you want to get money. Diamonds are business money cards; they're good for luxury, teaching, public speaking, even writing. This would be a good time to try different avenues, different ways of doing business. Have you ever played around with writing a book? This would be a time for a very good beginning; you have good ideas here.

Tess: This is the communication house.

Sophia: Yes, that's right. It also can be computer and high-tech stuff, but it would be the development or learning of these things. The eleventh house is more of the accomplishment of this. Use this card to your advantage, it's a good one. One word of caution, though: you don't always trust others. With the queen of spades next to this card, you don't trust this woman.

The fourth house has the two of spades, so life at home has not been the most comfortable for you recently. The two of spades shows that, for example, you're doing some work on your home, such as remodeling, and it's turning out to be more of a mess than you thought it would be. You want to ask, "Why doesn't this disappear?" It's not a huge annoyance, it doesn't consume you, but it's something you think about. Like a minor inconvenience, but being a spade it's uncomfortable and in the fourth house it's something in your home. I bet you're a little angry at a family member.

Tess: Yes, this is true.

Sophia: You have a jack of clubs in the fifth house, so this is someone whom you spend your free time with. Jacks are usually younger men, or it could be a woman, but it would be a very assertive woman. A "kick-ass" girl. The jack of clubs is just somebody who is more intense and, being in the fifth house, they are also a lot of fun. Somebody that you go out and do things with and enjoy. Looking at the cards around you, it's clear that you have not gone out and enjoyed yourself in a long time, that you have not gone to a movie, theater, or out to dinner. In short, you have not gone out and done much at all that is fun.

Tess: True, true, true.

Sophia: The jack of clubs would be your escort. This person would convince you to go out with them. Why not take him or her up on the offer? This person knows how to have a good time. Why not go out and party? You'll have fun.

With the seventh of clubs in the sixth house, you have so much work to do, more then you normally have. It seems that every time you have completed something, you have more that needs to be done. With the seven of clubs, it's easy to feel overwhelmed. I'll bet that at this time many people are asking you to do things for them; you're spending your time trying to decide what is the best way to reach out to others and help yourself at the same time.

Tess: So true.

Sophia: Here in the seventh house (pointing at card) you have the ten of clubs. You're questioning relationship things right now. The ten of clubs means you have been working on a relationship or partnership for a long time. Now you're looking at it differently. The good thing about a ten is that it's almost done. Because it's such a high number, it will turn into a face card or another suit soon. This wondering and working on a relationship is either with business or marriage. It's now healing, getting better, and softening.

Tess: I think this must be business, because everything is evolving nicely.

Sophia: Good, that makes sense, because what this card is saying is that you have been working so hard for so long that everything is going to turn out great. You have had your nose to the grindstone for so long, working within a unit. Now things will turn out just wonderfully. What I would suggest, looking back here at the jack, is that you should contact this person and go out and have a good time. You have earned a celebration.

Tess: I have done enough! You're right!

Sophia: Yes, you have. The eighth house has the eight of spades, which indicates that everything is a little more intense here with the double eights. This signifies other people who have a direct effect on you. Interpreting the cards, I would say that you're worried about another person. The card is pointing at the second house; you're worried about another person and their money. This affects you a lot. This person may cost you money. Do you have anybody that you send money to? Somebody that you help? They may even ask you for more money; it's a dark woman.

Tess: I know who that is.

Sophia: You're questioning your personal philosophy right now. Not yourself, but your values. Looking at a layout like this shows you're thinking a lot about the future.

Tess: Yes, I am also thinking about the present.

Sophia: You're processing an amazing amount tossing away old beliefs and bringing in some new ones. Interesting though, everything you're thinking about is very serious. You're in an extremely serious mood right now with the two of clubs in the ninth house. It's not the best time to take any kind of major trip. It's better to live life slowly and absorb all that is around you. Don't let others take advantage of you. Also, looking back at the seven of clubs, you have some major health issues. You're trying to take over your own health care and not leave it in the hands of others. You're taking back what you want.

Tess: Yes.

Sophia: In the tenth house you have the three of spades. Twos and threes are so minor that they are just the beginning of a new cycle. Being spades, they are difficulties. With the three of spades, you're wondering if this is the right career path for you or maybe you're about to try something new in business. Looking at this, though, shows that you're stressed out at work and have millions of tiny details you have to work with. This card is also telling you to look at your career in a realistic fashion.

Looking at this reading, I would say this has been a tough fall season for you.

Tess: Yes, it has. You're right in many ways.

Sophia: In the eleventh house, you have the nine of clubs so friends have been asking too much from you and they are wearing you down. You're starting to fight back a little by not letting others push you around. Don't get angry at them because you don't stick up for yourself. The card also indicates your creativity, which is not a driving force in your life right now.

Tess: Is that ever true.

Sophia: A lot of changes, a lot of difficulties, a lot of disappointment. But your spirit is soaring in the twelfth house with the ace of hearts! You really can't get a better card. So much love in your home. Love with your family, but with the other stuff going on you're saying, "Gee, inside I feel great but the outside things are not going as well as expected." This card represents your subconscious, but the cards that surround you don't match such a positive attitude. The cards that are high numbers are nearing transition—they will probably change for the better. Since the cards are only good for two or three weeks, everything will start to improve around the holidays.

In the future, your cards will more likely be diamonds and hearts. With the lower spade numbers, twos and threes, you will probably be working on changes in your home and business. Pay attention to the person in the second house; she has been hanging on and has been asking too much of you. You have more responsibility for her than you want.

Tess: Yes, I know who that is and, she is insatiable.

Sophia: Yes, but everything will get better. Now do you have questions?

Tess: No, this pretty much is what has been going on.

Sophia: The cards are interesting that way. They are great at explaining the energy around you. You're sure you don't have any questions?

Tess: No, not really. You hit just about everything!

Sophia: What is interesting is that you have the ace of hearts in the twelfth house. This means your subconscious is great; I bet your counseling sessions are very insightful and people love them. You have much power now, but it doesn't reflect what is going on at all.

Tess: Interesting, very interesting. True, I think.

Sophia: This shows that you can rise above adversity that you make the most of what you have.

Tess: So this one (points to the eleventh house) has to do with friendships, that is what you said.

Sophia: Yes, friendships and trying to reach someone important, such as a mentor; but judging by the card it's more of a friendship. It's the higher mind working, but in the realm of creativity. Look at this card; you probably can write well and have much to share with others, although, since it's a nine of clubs I doubt that you will be starting any new projects.

Tess: I have enough projects.

Sophia: Yes, with the two and three here you don't need to take on any more; it's more beneficial to start to delete things. Look at the tenth house; you're trying to do more to increase long-term goals. When I read this card, I noticed you're revamping quite a bit. What you want now is different from your past.

Tess: This is interesting because I have been thinking of sitting down and writing down my values. Not only do I want to get my values clearer, I want to be clear about my life, my priorities now. Right now I need to know where to put my energy. I am so scattered; there are so many demands on me right now. Everything is not being settled, like the newsletter. Two classes got scheduled at the same time. I don't know where this happened and two people have conflicts in schedules; one is going out of town, the other decided not to teach anymore. I have deadlines that are coming up and I haven't even started yet. So my world is mad!

Sophia: Yes, you can see with the nine of clubs that you're doing so much for other people, but it does not seem to be doing much for you. Most of your cards are work cards and they are pulling you in many directions at once. There is work on your health, partnership, long-term goals, working on your values. You just decided to do everything the same day. (Both laugh!)

Tess: It's so typical of me. All right, this is so interesting.

Sophia: Yes, it is. I would tell you, though, that it's important to go out and have a good time with the jack of clubs.

Tess: I'm not sure who this is.

Sophia: Jacks can be women, but they are assertive women; she has brown hair and hazel eyes. The jack of clubs are the classic yuppie type; they are youthful and know what they want out of life.

Tess: Oh, now I know who you're talking about. Well, she tends to tell me her problems.

Sophia: With the cards that surround her, this is true. You have enough going on with other people; don't take on any more problems. Especially other people's. But she's in a place to just have fun with now.

Tess: Really? I need to start to set up some boundaries and I need to enjoy.

Sophia: Do you want to make a wish at all? Just pick a card, any card, and I will tell you if your wish will come through.

Tess: I have more than one.

Sophia: Then we'll pull more than one card. Let's see, the first card is the five of spades, which means work. You take control of the situation.

Tess: That's what I'm doing.

Sophia: The answer is yes, but it's a work one. The next card is the seven of hearts—a yes, definitely.

Tess: Good, I wished for happiness and contentment. Seven and three are my numbers! Great, thank you so much.

Sample Reading: Julie

This young single woman had just started a new career and was looking to buy a condominium. She was also interested in finding a mate.

Sophia: Interesting. The first house is the queen of spades. Usually, this means you, but it also could be someone that you're dealing with who is very intense. She is dark and strong; it could be a man. I can tell by looking at this card and the cards around it that it's not a man; it must be a woman.

Julie: Yes, I know who you're talking about.

Sophia: The two of spades in the second house. Your money is not what you want it to be at all. It's preventing you from doing a lot and hindering what you want to do with your life. This is the house of money. With the two of spades, you're saying to yourself, "Hey, what else can I do to make it better?" The two of spades is the beginning of that realization. You realize your money is all right—but it's really not all right; it is concern for long-term planning and not achieving what you want.

Julie: True.

Sophia: You have the seven of clubs in the third house. That card represents teaching and communication. You have been working hard on getting your voice heard. You have been working hard to get somewhere;

such as finding the work you want to do. Some of your ideas, though, are a little unrealistic.

Julie: Oh, yes.

Sophia: Ace of spades in the fourth house is your home. Major changes within your home. Are you going to move? Or are you going to radically change something in the home? Maybe it's at a point that everything has changed so much that it's not worth staying still anymore.

Julie: I want to buy a house or condominium, but that gets back to number two here. (Laughs.) Never enough resources!

Sophia: Well, the ace of spades is a wild card, only it means the end. Then something changes; but it might be for the better. It would be a big deal, such as buying a condo. Are you looking now? Something big is coming in that area.

Julie: Yes, I have been looking for the past month. I will be starting to look even more seriously soon; I have been checking markets. I am mostly worried about resale so that is why I might wait. I would rather be in the city. Then you're talking a lot more money. Something will happen, we will see. It's my first major purchase.

Sophia: The fifth house has the four of hearts and so you're doing what you like to do; you're spending time with the people you like to spend time with. You're finding what you like to do and you're doing it. You're finding new ways of creative inspiration.

Julie: Exactly.

Sophia: You're enjoying being with others and going out a lot.

Julie: I have been having a lot of fun recently.

Sophia: The three of hearts in the sixth house is great. If you've noticed, you have the three of hearts next to the four of hearts and they are pointing at each other; actually they're touching. The combination of these two is that work is pleasurable and easy. When you have the fifth and sixth houses with cards that are so similar, you enjoy your work.

Julie: That is definitely true!

Sophia: What is interesting, though, is that you have an ace of clubs in your seventh house. This is relationships and it means that they are going to change for you.

Julie: Excellent. Boy, would that be nice.

Sophia: It's a big change, but a lot has to do with how you view relationships because this house with this card is indicating that you have work to do, especially with one-on-one relationships.

Julie: I can see that.

Sophia: The seven of spades in your eighth house shows that you're spending your time looking at possibilities for the future. I need to caution you, though, that this is not the best time to sign contracts or get involved with major financial manners. This card is not one for going ahead and investing; it's a card that's warning you to slow down. It's saying don't invest, don't do anything; just be a looker right now. This is a cautious card and it's giving you a good reason to be cautious; you don't have the resources to lose. Others may not be that honest with you, so don't sign any papers.

Julie: That makes sense from my financial state.

Sophia: Ninth house; you have the five of spades. This is traveling and buying books. Even if you're doing what you enjoy doing, you don't have the resources to do what you want to do, such as travel long distances, take classes, or go back to school. Higher education is not feasible right now. This bothers you. It's like feeling short-changed. Actually, this woman in the first house might help you.

Julie: True! This is amazing!

Sophia: Career issues in the tenth house have the four of diamonds. Your career is moving slower then you desire. Only you're on the right track!

Julie: Good, that's great. Now maybe that will help my two of spades here.

Sophia: That is true. It's like a springboard. You say to yourself, "Well, I'm doing all this work and trying so hard." You're enjoying yourself and your job is good. This is more of the feeling that you're being held back. You want more.

Julie: This is true. My career is typing envelopes, but I hope for more soon!

Sophia: Your career doesn't look bad; you're probably paid okay for what you do. The people are nice, too.

Julie: It's more money then I have ever earned and I just love the people, they are all so nice. After my last job, all I can do is go up.

Sophia: The ten of spades in the eleventh house shows you have concerns about some friends. Some long-term plans you had together didn't work out.

Julie: Oh, yes.

Sophia: Some of your friends are having a very hard time. They are telling you their problems. Maybe dumping on you?

Julie: So true!

Sophia: The ten of diamonds in the twelfth house shows you're looking at the world very optimistically now. You have belief in yourself and believe that you can have what you want. Long term or short term, you can get what you want out of life.

Julie: Interesting. I think those things are right.

Sophia: Do you have questions about the cards?

Julie: No, that was great. You got everything, thank you so much. Oh, one question, who is that in the first house?

Sophia: It's yourself or somebody who has such a great influence over you that they can make major decisions for you. You being a blond, I doubt this is you and judging by the cards around it, especially with the ace of spades in the fourth house, it may be an elderly relative, who is ill, and has money or some type of hold over you.

Julie: My grandmother just found out yesterday that she is diabetic. But I have another grandmother who is healthy. It makes sense; one has a house that she is thinking of selling, I could benefit from that and we are close. Now what were you saying about the ace of clubs?

Sophia: Well, the ace of clubs is a change in a relationship or business partnership. It's more of a change at how you look at relationships. Since you don't have a jack or king in your reading, you can't look at one person who is changing your view of relationship. The viewpoint comes from within and you're looking at relationships much more definitely. The aces are wild cards so you can't control the energy. So what house is this in? The seventh. So, your home; big changes coming. You have many nice cards in your reading; you also have some strong cards that make everything more difficult. Definitely, it's a bittersweet reading. You will have change because of the combination of the two. You will also have change in your home; I bet you will move.

Julie: Correct. This is what is happening in my life now; it has become stable, but I want more. The intellectual part of my life is gone. I just finished a class in pottery and I will be taking another one. Yes, something definite is going to have to change. I am disappointed that I can't travel and I would like to take more classes. I am very stable where I am, but on the other hand some of my needs are not being met.

Sophia: Yes, you have some interesting issues right now.

Julie: It's a very transitional time right now.

Sophia: Take a card, any card, and I will tell you if your wish will come true.

Julie: Great, let's see. Now what was I going to say? Oh, I'm so worried about relationships; it's my biggest worry. Here's my card.

Sophia: Of course!

Julie: Oh cool, I am going to end up with a great relationship.

Sophia: Yes, with a nice man.

Julie: Really? Who?

Sophia: This is the king of diamonds and he is a real person, do you want me to tell you about him?

Julie: You can? Tell me please.

Sophia: He is fair-haired, not a blond but more of a dark blond. He has money and good self-esteem. He is not someone who is starting out in life, but one who has already finished his schooling and is well into his career. He is mature, people like him and he is well respected.

Others look up to him. He is always a professional. If he is a plumber, he would own ten plumbing stores and would manage them. He has a strong personality and a great character. So there you go.

Julie: Cool, well, interesting. Maybe Santa will bring me something good.

Sophia: Remember, you will have changes in your home, so watch out. The cards in the fourth and seventh houses indicate changes. Be careful of any home accidents. Spades are a warning, so don't space out and leave any lights on your Yule Tree or candles burning. Be careful the next couple of weeks. Low numbers mean that things will remain the same for a while, higher numbers show it will change soon.

Julie: Excellent, this was so much fun. Thank you.

Sophia: You're welcome.

As you can see, to interpret the cards using this Wheel of Life spread is really very simple. To improve your skills, read astrological books for more on the houses and spend your time reading cards every week. Pick one day to be your "reading day" and practice on family and friends. It's also important to listen to what the person is saying about their reading and get feedback on how you're doing. Use your intuition; the cards are flexible and will speak to you. Notice how the meanings can be adjusted as they lie near other cards. Most of all, enjoy it. It's fun. You will also be surprised; the cards are accurate to predict the future and to see the outcome you will have for yourself as well as for others.

CHAPTER 7

The Grand Star Spread

The Grand Star spread is a card reading system I learned long ago. This fun-to-use spread is a traditional French way to read the cards.

The card layout for this spread is interesting and usually amazes people. Although it can be tricky to remember what card is read first, it does not take long to get the hang of it. One reason this spread is so popular and has survived for so long is that it is very personal. The reader selects the card that looks the most like the person he or she is giving the reading for. For example, if your client is a blond-haired, blue-eyed woman who is maternal and warm, you would pick the queen of hearts. (The Sophia deck of cards is easier to use for this purpose because the cards are in tune with people's physical features. You choose the card that is best for the reading and will look like you have more insight.)

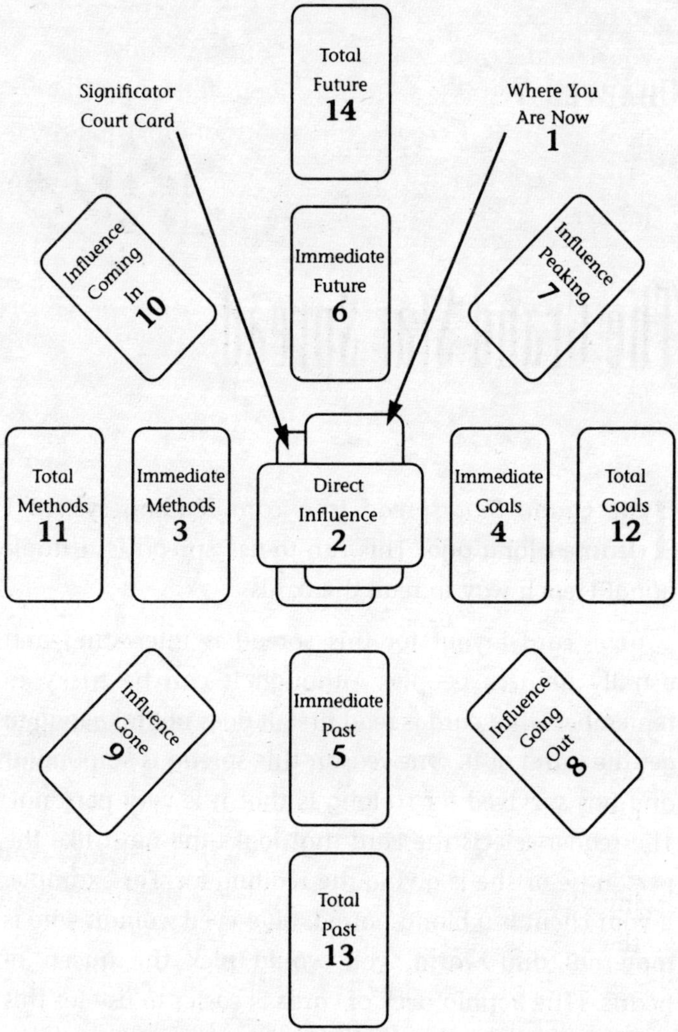

Fig. 4– The Grand Star spread

To begin the Grand Star spread, shuffle the cards until you feel they are mixed and you are ready. Place the cards on the table in front of you, following the order in the illustration. Use the information in chapter 2, "The Meanings of the Cards," to read the cards in the layout.

A card is placed in the center, it is a face card that represents the client (or you); it is sometimes called a "significator." It is chosen by the reader to represent the client (or self). You can see how to do this by referring to the descriptions of each face card in the book.

The first card of the reading, placed on top of the face card, represents where the person is now, their (or your) current state of being.

The second card horizontally covers the first card and is the immediate influence on the individual; where you are at now.

The third card on the left side is for immediate methods; it represents how the person is trying to accomplish his or her objectives right now.

The fourth card on the right side of the face card is immediate goals. This card shows the short-term goal of the individual.

The fifth card, directly below the first card, represents the immediate past (within the past week or two).

The sixth card is directly above the first card and is the immediate future; it represents something that will happen within the next week or two.

Cards seven through ten are the influences that are outside the life of the individual. These cards are similar to the four phases of the moon.

The seventh card is placed on the right side of the sixth card; it represents the full moon or an influence peaking.

The eighth card is placed between the fifth and fourth cards; it is similar to the moon waning, or an influence that is going out.

The ninth card is placed between the third and fifth cards; it represents an outside influence that is completely gone; similar to the dark of the moon.

The tenth card is located between the third and fourteenth cards; it represents the moon increasing. This card indicates a new influence coming in.

The eleventh card is placed near the third card and reveals the total methods a person uses to get what he or she wants.

The twelfth card is placed next to the fourth card and represents the total long-term, overall goals of the individual.

The thirteenth card, the total past card, is placed below the fifth card. It shows how the individual's year has gone.

The fourteenth card is placed above the sixth card. It is the total long-term future card; it is the individual's future for about a year.

This layout looks lovely and is extremely accurate. The Grand Star spread has survived centuries. As with other readings, keep in mind that the cards influence each other. For example, if the immediate future card (the sixth card) shows a new project and the influences peaking card (the seventh card) shows money, a project coming along will pay well.

Sample Reading: Jeff

Jeff is a talented artist who is on his way to success. As you can see in his reading, however, he has sacrificed a great deal to get where he is today. (I first laid out the King of Spades to symbolize Jeff. Then I began the reading.)

Sophia: The first card is where you are now, and you have the seven of spades, which is about taking risks. It also means that you have had many difficulties for some time. The seven is a high number so you have been working at these difficulties for a while. Spades are like obstacles; you see this suit when you have been striving for something or trying to work things out. Looking at where the card is, I would say that you have been questioning yourself for a while about something you have been working toward, something that you desire.

Jeff: Can I touch the cards?

Sophia: By all means.

Jeff, looking at the Sophia deck: This is incredible. These cards are very unusual and very interesting.

Sophia: Thank you. They are lovely are they not? The next card is what is crossing you and is the immediate influence in your life (the eight of Clubs).

Jeff: You mean in the bad sense of the word.

Sophia: No. This card is the key influence on you right now. With the eight of clubs showing, you have wanted to achieve something for a while—which is your immediate influence. It shows much work. Whatever you're undertaking right now, it has been a result of much work.

Jeff: Yes, that's right.

Sophia: The next is your immediate methods, which is the nine of hearts. You know what you want; you want love and this is the method you use to get what you need in life. You're very emotive. If you do not totally care about what you're doing, heart and soul, you probably won't stick with it. Surrounding yourself with good, intelligent friends and love is shown with the nine of hearts. How you go about manifesting your dreams in life is entirely feasible.

Jeff: That is good news.

Sophia: The next card is your immediate goals, what you want. The king of clubs here shows you are collaborating with a man with brown hair and hazel to brown eyes. The king of clubs can also appear quite dark. He helps you with what you need. He is goal-oriented and a strong individual. He has a definite personality. He can be very intense.

Jeff: Is he someone who would be involved with criminal activities?

Sophia: Oh, no, no, no. I mean dark in coloring or a serious personality. The king of clubs is a helpful person you would want on your side as a good friend.

Jeff: I now know who he is.

Sophia: Your next card is your immediate past—which would be in the past week or two—and it is the nine of clubs so you recently had a major ordeal. Things have been tough for you, but now you realize that they are past. It was not a misfortune. It was a problem that has been around for a while. Now your problems are starting to be resolved.

Jeff: Interesting. It's really true.

Sophia: The immediate future here shows that you have a totally opposite card, the nine of diamonds. This card is money, good luck, great things happening to you in the immediate future. A real change, from nine to nine!

Jeff: Great, I'm going to move this card closer to me.

Sophia (laughs): Sure, go ahead. In the next couple of weeks you will be on to something big. You're leaving dark times behind. With the nine of diamonds in the immediate future, you're headed for some good luck. It looks like you have some major projects that you're working on that should generate money.

Jeff: Well, actually I am.

Sophia: The next is the seven of clubs; this is influences peaking. This means that you have a lot of work still ahead of you, but it will work out to your favor. It is important to reflect on any plans; you'll do everything with passion and dedication.

Jeff, pointing to the king of clubs: It is related to this card. This is the guy who is dark and has a strong influence on me.

Sophia: Yes. All the cards in a reading are related. You have to look at all of them. The next card is influences going out. With the jack of spades, it would be a young man or woman who is assertive. Soon, that person will no longer be an influence; the relationship is resolving. It would be your girlfriend I bet, looking at the other cards. Spade cards are people who are darker in complexion than the clubs. Would this be her?

Jeff: That's what I think. That it's her.

Sophia: Like I said, she is going out; it is the resolving of your relationship.

Jeff: We finally broke up, it's finished.

Sophia: Oh! Well, that's it then. The following card is an influence that is gone, it really is over. With the seven of diamonds here, it seems that this has cost you something, such as money or even your home. Great self-sacrifices have been made. In many ways, you have a new look outside and inside.

Jeff: This is an influence that's gone? Good! Because it makes sense. She now has the apartment, and it cost a lot of money to set myself up again. Because it is diamonds it has to do with money, wealth, or possessions? And being a high number it shows a lot of sacrifices?

Sophia: Right. With the nine of clubs right next to it, the two cards are closely related and show how things will work out. The next couple of weeks will be interesting.

Jeff: I'll say. What is the next one?

Sophia: An influence coming in with the queen of diamonds. Now this person has light hair and light eyes. She is generous, open, and very helpful. She will be a major influence in your life. The queen of diamonds wants to help, wants somebody to help you give the queen a call. It is her nature to want to help. She is a great person.

Jeff: This is making sense. I know her.

Sophia: The cards all mean something; it is all starting to work out. They would not have survived since the thirteenth century if they weren't accurate!

Jeff: All the bugs have been worked out, hmm?

Sophia: I have seen a book with this same spread from the twenties—who knows how long it has been around? I have seen great card readers use this spread. The next card is the nine of spades in the place of total methods.

This is not the easiest card; in the past a reader would have told you that you're surrounded by deep sorrow. This simply is not true; today we have much more control over our lives. This card means you have picked a path that is difficult but not impossible; it's challenging. The prize that you can achieve is unbelievably great.

Jeff: As a professional artist, nothing is truly easy.

Sophia: The next is total goals. With the six of spades, your goals are not easy and it will take some time to get what you want. The goals may change, but ultimately they will be obtainable. The cards are all related so you need to look at this as a whole.

Sophia: Next is the total past, which is the two of clubs. Something in the past has not worked out. With the two of clubs here, you still can carry some of the same ideas that have held you back in the past, but now you're forging ahead. This means that you have given up the connection that has held you back in your past. You have broken with the total past which, I should add, is the past year or so. It has been a slow time coming to where you are.

Jeff: Yeah. What's next; what is this card?

Sophia: Total love. In the last card, the total future is the seven of hearts. You love what you do and you love where you're going. Life will improve greatly for you this year. Many times, it reunites you with a past love.

Jeff (laughs, relieved.)

Sophia: Looking at the whole reading, I can see that you've earned all you've worked for. You have many sevens in your reading.

Jeff: What does seven mean?

Sophia: That you're about to hit your stride to do your ultimate best. For many people, the number seven is very lucky. Lucky number seven. Sevens are a good number in the cards, too. Your reading is a mixed bag; it is definitely a time of highs and lows for you. You've had rough struggles and broken with several past people and things. Your sacrifices will begin to pay off soon. Your work is going to take you into many new territories that you'll find challenging and hard. It is going to be successful. A month ago, you wouldn't have thought that what you'd be going to do is something that is about to be done. This queen of diamonds is going to do much for you; she is going to start to bring some money in.

Jeff: Yes, she is going to start to bring some money in. Already she has been bringing corporations into my studio to see about purchasing some of my paintings.

Sophia: Do you have any future questions?

Jeff: No, thank you so much; it really was helpful.

Sample Reading: Susan

This lovely woman is a single mother who has a very intense job. She is a gifted teacher and can inspire anyone to learn. (I put the queen of clubs down as a significator.)

Sophia: We are going to use the Grand Star card layout. I think it is the most beautiful one. Doesn't it look nice?

Susan: Yes, it is very nice looking.

Sophia: It is interesting as well as pretty. I like this spread a lot and it is practical too. Hmm. The ten of clubs is where you are now. You're near the completion of your work. You have had a lot of work; the ten of clubs shows that you're relieved that you have reached the top of what you needed to achieve. You have reached your goal—a recent occurrence. Clubs are work so it has to do with the finishing up of a project.

Susan: Yes! My students are just finishing up.

Sophia: Since your students have finished their program, you have reached the end of your goal. You're saying, "I've finished my classes; I'm done." The next card is the seven of clubs, which is directly covering you. You still see a lot of work to do, even though you're technically finished. The seven of clubs is the direct influence covering you. It does not mean that you have really finished. Actually the paperwork from your job is ever larger because you have finished your work; you still have some loose ends. I bet you tend to think that if you had to do things over again you just might.

Susan (Laughs): I still haven't posted my grades and the students ask me when I'll finish.

Sophia: Here. Your immediate method is how you go about doing things. With the ace of hearts here, you throw yourself passionately into whatever you're doing. Ace energy is hard to control; it is a wild card and hearts are love so you direct much passion and throw yourself into situations. You're pretty optimistic; that is how you go about doing things. You say when starting a new situation. "Oh, I would love to do that; I would be so good at it." You're very enthusiastic.

Susan: True, true, true.

Sophia: The next card is your immediate goals, and that is the ten of spades. With the ten of spades, you're looking at what you want to achieve and sometimes you wonder if what you want to do is really feasible. You're not pessimistic, just clear when you look at your goals and wonder if they're realistic. You wonder about the same thing over and over again, saying to yourself, "Is this the right move for me?"

The next card shows the immediate past, and with the four of spades you have spent much time wondering how you're going to achieve what you want. Sometimes your desires have been slow in fruition. The past week or so I would say that you've had some obstacles and minor inconveniences. The immediate past is the past week or two, which has not been the easiest for you.

Susan: Everything in my life is now starting to make more sense. I can see it clearly now.

Sophia: The immediate future is the six of clubs; again this is this week and next, rarely would it spill further than that. The six of clubs is a procrastinating card. You have needed to move along in some sort of direction, and you really haven't done anything one way or another.

Susan: This is very true—you should see my desk both at home and work.

Sophia: Oh, a people card is next. You have the jack of hearts, which is in the influences peaking place. He has a great influence over you. Many times, this card can represent a woman, but usually it is a man with light hair and light eyes, who's fun-loving. This person has much influence over you right now—especially concerning some goals and something you want. Your future and goals have a lot to do with this one person. This is really a go-getter type of person.

Susan: This is so interesting. I know who he is.

Sophia: The influences going out card is the five of hearts. Everything seems to be easier for you. Right now is a good time to enjoy what you have and what you like. This card is telling you that things are going to be getting harder soon, that you're going to have more work in the future. Now you have a lull; the calm before the storm. The five of hearts is a fun card; it's telling you to go out and do the things that you enjoy. Enjoy movies, the theater, restaurants, or whatever brings you pleasure. This is a good time to take advantage of those things that you enjoy doing. Maybe a date?

Susan: I have a few weeks before my new students arrive here from Japan.

Sophia: Next is influences that are gone, which is the five of diamonds. Money seemed to come to you pretty easily, but now it is harder for you to make it as easily as you used to. The diamond suit means money and this card is in a place where influences are gone—where money came easily in the past, it now is no longer true. It is much more difficult for you to save money, too.

Susan: Yes, I'm near the end of my child support payments. Yes, that's true. My son's father no longer gives me money. Resources become less.

Sophia: Influence coming in is the three of clubs. You have a lot of petty work coming your way. You're ending some major projects and then you're going to get very busy again; doing something at work that is really not that enjoyable for you. I would take advantage of the cards that tell you to have a good time. With the three of clubs here, it seems that it is going to be another long year of struggling up to the top. Better enjoy yourself while the time is right.

The next card, in the total methods space, is the ace of clubs. You're working very hard and feverishly to get what you want and you don't slack off. You have very good luck. You overwork yourself though. The methods card, the way you go about getting things, is great. Because you have two aces here, you throw yourself into high ideas. Nothing is too idealistic for you; nothing is too hard. You really launch yourself with total love into whatever you do.

Susan: This is true.

Sophia: The total goals card is the five of spades. Again, that means something that you thought you would get really did not materialize the way you thought it would. In the beginning, things seemed better than they turned out to be. Things have changed for you a little bit, and when that happens it shocks you.

Next is the total past, which has the four of hearts in it. This is the past year and it seems that life was a little bit easier or more optimistic than it is now. Expectations were rosier. It is probable that now—after living here for a year, seeing what this city is like, and getting used to your job—you have a realistic view of what's expected of you and what will unfold in the coming year. With the four of hearts here, I bet you had a pretty good year.

Susan: I had a good year; but it seems harder now, you're right.

Sophia: Your total future card is the two of hearts, which is the beginning of wonderful things coming to you. In the total past, you've looked at goals or desires concerning what you have wanted; you've gone after what you've needed. Now you're starting off on new goals. You've formed these new ideas, goals, and things that you've wanted to do, so you've started creating your base. You've built up your foundation and now you know what works and what doesn't work. Now you know what you want to take on to reach your next step. You have different ideas and dreams than you did last year. Last year, it was more survival: secure a home, be successful in your job, get a car, get your son set up in school, and so on. Now you've done all that and are successful in surviving a lot of learning, a lot of ups and down, and an exploration of relationships. Now things are really changing for you.

That is the difference now that you've completed a lot of work. Now things are going to start to get better, in a better way. You have different goals now. You've told me what you want, that you desire a house. You're going to move on to new goals and I know you'll be successful at it. Your goals are realistic. You will have some setbacks, but they will tell you that it is not impossible—there are always a few difficult things. Do you have any questions?

Susan: Yes. I forgot, what does this card mean and the one that is crossing over it?

Sophia: The ten of clubs is where you're at now; and the one that's crossing it is your immediate influence. The ten of clubs is a completion card; you have finished your work. The card covering it is the seven and it means you have more work to do. The grading, remember? So your immediate influence is that even though you've finished your work, you don't feel like you did.

Susan: That is true. All of it is true! Thank you; that was a great reading.

CHAPTER 8

The Master Spread

My grandmother favored the Master spread (she wasn't, after all, a great fan of astrology). This is an all-encompassing spread, one that takes a long time to use and results in a long, involved reading. In the diagram, you'll notice all the attributes and positions of the reading; but even so it will take some time to get the hang of this spread. The joy of the Master spread is its thoroughness; it really tells you how your life is going—all of it.

Another joy of using the Master spread is that, if you are interested in only a partial reading, you do not need to turn over every card. When my grandmother had personal questions of a specific nature, she would only turn over the first six cards to see how something would turn out. In readings, I have often seen only the first twelve cards exposed. Even with a partial reading, it is still important to use the same layout.

My husband refers to this partial reading as "psychic card reading pull tabs." In a way, he is right, but you have to remember that if you only pull one card in the middle, say number twenty-two, without looking at the other cards around it, the meaning is shallow. You may think you have a grasp of the situation, but you really do not. If you are doing a partial reading and want general information, stick with the tradition of looking at the first six or twelve cards together.

In the Master spread, the suit will always bring to mind the same ideas, which makes reading the cards not only more accurate, but also easier to understand as well.

- Hearts are almost always love, romance, good luck, and great happiness. Even if the card is surrounded by unfortunate cards, the hearts are similar to a ray of sun through a rain cloud.
- Diamonds are the money card and show loyal and giving friends, it is a fortunate card to have in case of a difficult card around it. A diamond means that, chances are, the friends in your life will bail you out.
- Clubs are the workers of the playing card deck; you need them to help achieve long-term goals. They can also indicate a difficult beginning.
- Spades are obstacles in life—things that make life difficult for you. The good part about spades is that they make you strong; spades are not for whimps.

Projects in Hand 1	Satis-fation 2	Success 3	Hope 4	Chance and Luck 5	Wishes and Desire 6
Injustice 7	Ingra-titude 8	Business Associa-tion 9	Loss 10	Trouble 11	State or Condition 12
Joy and Delight 13	Love 14	Prosperity 15	Marriage 16	Depression or Sorrow 17	Pleasure and Enjoyment 18
Inherited Money or Property 19	Fraud or Deceit 20	Rivals 21	A Gift 22	A Lover 23	Advan-cement 24
Kindness 25	Under-taking and Enterprise 26	Changes 27	Death 28	Reward 29	Misfor-tune 30
Happiness 31	Money and Fortune 32	Indiffe-rence 33	Favor 34	Ambition 35	Poor Health 36

Fig. 5– The Master spread

To begin the Master spread, shuffle the cards and cut the deck into three piles. Place the cards face down, starting with the left corner (marked number one in the illustration). Continue with all the cards until you have filled the thirty-six squares. Turn each card over and read one individually. Pay attention to each card's position.

Following is the formula that gives a general overview on each position by suit. Look at the meaning of each card and take into account how the suit fits each position in this spread.

Number one: Represents the individual getting the reading.

Hearts: Good influence; projects started now will be successful.

Diamonds: Others will help you with your needs.

Clubs: Serious problems involving you and others.

Spades: You find it difficult to trust.

Number two: Satisfaction.

Hearts: Contentment of life's path; realization of hope and desires.

Diamonds: Wonderful help through life; someone will give you boundless support.

Clubs: Envy and jealousy can stop you from feeling satisfied; others may control you.

Spades: Deceit will stop you from feeling complete; fight this double-crossing.

Number three: Success.

Hearts: It seems that success is yours for the taking.

Diamonds: Friends will help you succeed.

Clubs: Success will be incomplete; projects are unfinished.

Spades: Very little chance for success; it will be destroyed by an underhanded mess.

Number four: Hope.

Hearts: Searching for the fulfillment of hope.

Diamonds: Many friends are very supportive of your aspirations and hopes.

Clubs: Unrealistic in what you hope to obtain brings much disappointment.

Spades: Wild fantastic hopes that push you off center cause trouble or tragedy.

Number five: Chance and Luck.

Hearts: Good luck with plans and goals; you can achieve a lot right now.

Diamonds: Moderately good luck, especially with money or material goods.

Clubs: Not very good luck; best not to start anything new.

Spades: Bad luck; a disaster is near—beware of accidents.

Number six: Wishes and Desire.

Hearts: Fulfillment of wishes, especially if surrounded by other good cards.

Diamonds: Not all, but some wishes will come true in an unusual way.

Clubs: Even with your best effort, you will have only moderate success.

Spades: Disappointment and an absence of desires being fulfilled.

Number seven: Injustice.

Hearts: Any injustice done to you in the past will be undone to your advantage.

Diamonds: The injustice that has happened will take a long battle to repair.

Clubs: Not everything will turn out the way you want it to, but some things will go your way.

Spades: Serious misfortune; do not get involved with any contracts or lawsuits at this time if it can be avoided.

Number eight: Ingratitude.

Hearts: You now have the advantage in all ideas that you pursue.

Diamonds: Your friends and family come to your support in a time of need.

Clubs: Do not let others take advantage of you; put up a fight.

Spades: People do not see your true worth and can demand too much of you.

Number nine: Business association.

Hearts: Best results in business; great time to go in on a partnership.

Diamonds: Cooperation of coworkers or business partners are favorable.

Clubs: Caution and diplomacy will need to be used—and still the results are not great.

Spades: No benefits right now for you; your business partners or coworkers benefit from association with you.

Number ten: Loss.

Hearts: Loss of a loved one who helped you for a long time.

Diamonds: Loss of money and property; be careful of losing any treasured jewelry items.

Clubs: Loss of close friends and broken dreams.

Spades: Even your best intentions will be overlooked; serious compromises are your best option.

Number eleven: Trouble.

Hearts: Problems for others near and dear to you; you will need to console them.

Diamonds: Financial problems and surprise expenses will cost you money.

Clubs: Your friends will cause you grief and anxiety.

Spades: Troubles are caused from jealousy.

Number twelve: State or Condition.

Hearts: Life is improving, you are on the upswing.

Diamonds: You need the help of others to attain your goals; a couple of good friends go a long way.

Clubs: A lot of hard work ahead; nothing comes easy. You must fight your way to the top.

Spades: All goes from bad to worse; it is nearly impossible to get ahead right now.

Number thirteen: Joy and Delight.

Hearts: Pure joy and delight; the bluebird of happiness will come and visit you.

Diamonds: You find joy and material satisfaction in your life's work.

Clubs: Finally, all that you have worked for comes to bring you joy and delight.

Spades: After helping others for so long, it is your turn for supreme happiness, joy, and delight.

Number fourteen: Love.

Hearts: Fortunate in love, others love you and you return their love unconditionally.

Diamonds: Money and love go together, do not be too greedy. Your lover is honest.

Clubs: Love is trying and will be agitated by jealousy.

Spades: Beware of betrayal in love.

Number fifteen: Prosperity.

Hearts: The comforts of material possessions and money are surrounding you.

Diamonds: Luxury items and an expensive taste are here for you to enjoy with others.

Clubs: Moderate prosperity due to hard work and definite goals.

Spades: Serious problems; watch out for fraud or lawsuits. Be careful of investments.

Number sixteen: Marriage.

Hearts: A long happy marriage with much support and love.

Diamonds: Money and marriage—you probably need both to feel secure.

Clubs: Both you and your partner are pragmatic; good fortune.

Spades: It is wise to reconsider any marriage proposal at this time.

Number seventeen: Depression or Sadness.

Hearts: The clouds are about to be lifted and with the sadness disappearing from your life, there is a ray of hope.

Diamonds: Spending so much time thinking of your own problems will alienate you from others.

Clubs: Deep depression and sadness; you are finding it hard to make decisions about directions and goals.

Spades: Little faith in yourself and others will cause you to lose your way in life.

Number eighteen: Pleasure and Enjoyment.

Hearts: Bliss. Others love you and you return their love; you enjoy even the smallest of pleasures.

Diamonds: Time and money to enjoy all that you find fun; others enjoy your generosity.

Clubs: Finding time to relax and enjoy life is difficult for you; others inspire you to play.

Spades: It has been a long time since you have gone out and enjoyed yourself; negativity stops you every time.

Number nineteen: Inherited Money or Property.

Hearts: Possessions that have sentimental as well as monetary value will be given to you.

Diamonds: Family money and insurance money will give you the support you need to do what you want in this life.

Clubs: Fight for what is legally yours and learn the difference about what is not; you may be entitled to more than you think concerning inheritance.

Spades: Unless you start to read everything that you sign and pay attention to what is going on, you could lose a fortune.

Number twenty: Fraud or Deceit.

Hearts: Someone is trying to destroy you; they will be caught in their lies and prevented.

Diamonds: Look over the small print; you could lose money in a business deal.

Clubs: You are losing out on something that belongs to you because you are being too nice. Fight!

Spades: Major losses in any dealings; this will cost you a great deal and you will lose your good name and friends.

Number twenty-one: Rivals.

Hearts: Obtaining one's desire over others who try to stop you, no matter what they try to do.

Diamonds: Overcoming difficulties with the help of some friends; they protect you from rivals.

Clubs: Listen to your heart, others are telling you stories to their advantage.

Spades: Rivals will bring your downfall; others have warned you but you do not listen.

Number twenty-two: A Gift.

Hearts: A beautiful gift from a secret admirer; it is an unexpected present.

Diamonds: An expensive present with an unseen price attached to it; is it worth it?

Clubs: A labor of love—either it is a homemade present or someone gives you the priceless gift of an unusual present.

Spades: Turns out to be more responsibility than it is worth; may be best not to accept it.

Number twenty-three: A Lover.

Hearts: A wonderful, thoughtful, faithful lover. The strength of his or her love toward you can be overwhelming at the time.

Diamonds: Similar interests and goals; you both have good senses of humor and much love wherever you go.

Clubs: Either you work together or should; project-minded lovers get results.

Spades: The beloved will either be selfish, mean, vindictive, or all three. A bad combination.

Number twenty-four: Advancement.

Hearts: Soon you will see a rapid improvement in your worldly position, and it will exceed your wildest dreams.

Diamonds: Success is here! Long-term goals and dreams start to materialize and you achieve the advancement you want in life.

Clubs: After hard work for so many years, life is starting to pay off; you can reach your goals after all.

Spades: Try as you might, you are not getting anywhere; you need to rethink your plans and try harder.

Number twenty-five: Kindness. A Favor Is Returned.

Hearts: You will receive a favor that is beyond your expectation; it amazes you how kind some people can be.

Diamonds: Material goods or monetary favors are given to you as a result of past acts of kindness you have given others.

Clubs: A small act of kindness or an even smaller favor is offered; do not overlook the nature of the simplicity.

Spades: Others will break their promise of intentions that are never fulfilled. The favor is more of a lesson than a favor.

Number twenty-six: Undertaking and Enterprise.

Hearts: Whatever you decide to do will meet with great success as long as you follow your heart.

Diamonds: Great ideas will do well in any endeavor that involves money; success.

Clubs: Much more work than you originally thought there would be; success in the end.

Spades: Little planning and spiteful people will stop any project now before it starts.

Number twenty-seven: Changes.

Hearts: It is an auspicious time to consider a change; look around to see what is made available.

Diamonds: Change for the better will happen with the help of some friends.

Clubs: An attempt to change your life will be met with obstacles; it will be difficult to make progress.

Spades: As hard as you try to change, others try to hold you back from your true will—they make change almost impossible. Keep trying.

Number twenty-eight: Death.

Hearts: The death of a close relative or friend will bring you money or material goods.

Diamonds: You're in for some surprises due to a legacy from a friend or family member.

Spades: Your arch enemy is soon to depart from this sphere.

Clubs: Not the easiest way to get what you desire, but just the same it is now yours.

Number twenty-nine: Reward.

Hearts: You will be rewarded for all your past efforts, for helping others.

Diamonds: A fitting reward will be yours, if you persevere in your efforts.

Clubs: A well-deserved reward will be denied or reduced due to the smallness of others.

Spades: No reward, even if it is deserved; others take credit for your effort.

Number thirty: Misfortune.

Hearts: Nothing seems to work out at the present time—but misfortune will not stay forever.

Diamonds: Misfortune and some poor business deals will leave you high and dry; you will feel disgraced in front of your business associates.

Clubs: All that you have worked for will have misfortune; best to change horse in midstream.

Spades: Dishonesty and a poor attitude will cause disgrace, and it will be some time before things are restored to normal.

Number thirty-one: Happiness.

Hearts: Great happiness is on the way; it will be long lasting and satisfying. Others will ask you your secret.

Diamonds: A special friend helps you renew your faith in yourself and humanity.

Clubs: Happiness will appear in an unusual way—when you least expect it, something great will happen.

Spades: Others stand in the way of your heart's desire. You need to make changes to find happiness.

Number thirty-two: Money and Fortune.

Hearts: Money will come to you in great amounts if you do what you love in life.

Diamonds: Fortune and money are yours if you keep your ideals high and stop at nothing.

Clubs: Any money that you receive is from hard work and dedication.

Spades: Hold on to your money, do not let others talk you into parting with it for foolish investments.

Number thirty-three: Indifference.

Hearts: Confusion in what truly matters; you are indifferent to what really matters in life.

Diamonds: Indifference and lack of zest in what you do will have you lose the ability to enjoy life's pleasures.

Clubs: Giving yourself to others who are indifferent and unresponsive will cause a lot of grief.

Spades: Indifference to how you feel and how others feel as well will bring grief and loneliness.

Number thirty-four: Favor.

Hearts: Enjoyment of all that someone special gives.

Diamonds: Generous and magnanimous, you bestow on others and they give back to you.

Clubs: : Manipulating others for what you want can get the favors you want, for a price.

Spades: Unrealistic demands will get you nowhere; nobody owes you a thing in life.

Number thirty-five: Ambition.

Hearts: After putting so much work and drive into what you aspire to, you will have success.

Diamonds: Unrelenting drive and determination will get you far with your ambitions in life.

Clubs: Starting and stopping projects make everything much harder and stop you from realizing your potential.

Spades: Slow starts and a complicated path make achievement difficult, but never impossible.

Number thirty-six: Poor health.

Hearts: Being ill on again and off again will not cause any debilitating effects.

Diamonds: Trying alternatives for health may save your life.

Clubs: Working toward better health with diet and exercise helps in the long run.

Spades: Serious illness that may interfere with living a happy life.

Face Cards

As with other spreads, the face cards resemble people in your life. Where each card falls in a reading indicates that either the person has direct influence now in that area of life or will in the future. The strength of the influence is shown by what is next to the face card. If a card is behind the face card, it is in the past; in front of the face card, in the future; above the face card, outside influences; and below the face card, inside influences.

No matter what card is next to the face card, look to see what the other influences could be. If a face card is the first card drawn, then that card would not have a significant meaning past that which would influence you at this time. Following are the types of personalities and appearances.

King of Hearts: A blond-haired, blue-eyed, supportive, and loving individual; usually found in connection with love or romance.

When the king of hearts falls on square **2, 3, 4, 13, 14, 15, 16, 18, 19, 23, 24, 25, 29, 31, 32, 34, or 36:** a person who matches the description of the king of hearts would be the focus and would help realize the desires in respect to the meaning of the square.

When this card falls on square **1, 5, 6, 9, 12, 22, 26, 27, 28, or 35:** a resolution is helpful as long as the king is asked to assist in some manner.

When this card falls on unlucky squares **7, 8, 10, 11, 17, 20, 21, 30, or 33:** he is a person not to be trusted with whatever the square's meaning.

Queen of Hearts: A blond-haired, blue-eyed woman also connects with love or romance. This card has similar meaning to the king of hearts only with feminine energy.

When the queen of hearts falls on square **1, 3, 4, 5, 6, 9, 13, 19, 20, 24, 25, 26, or 34:** a woman matching this description will help.

When this card falls on square **2, 14, 15, 16, 18, 22, 23, 29, 31, 32, 35 or 36:** love is on the way to lift your spirits.

When the card falls on square **7, 8, 10, 11, 12, 17, 21, 27, 28, 30, or 33:** these reflect the meaning of the square, but in the context that the queen of hearts is someone who is more of a hindrance than a help.

Jack of Hearts: A young man or woman with blond hair and blue eyes; they are usually outgoing. More often than not the jack is a young man.

When the jack of hearts falls on square **1, 3, 5, 7, 9, 12, 19, 21, 24, 26, or 35**: a person who is your partner either in business or love would have a great deal of influence on you.

When the card falls on square **2, 4, 6, 10, 11, 13, 14, 15, 16, 18, 22, 23, 25, 27, 29, 31, or 34**: the jack of hearts would be an image of romance or the sheer pleasure of enjoyment, youthful love.

When the card falls on square **8, 17, 20, 28, 30, 32, 33, or 36**: no matter what number square the card lands on, keep in mind that the face card reflects the content of the meaning of the square. Jack of hearts is sometimes dependable and sometimes the person does not live up to your expectations.

King of Diamonds: A sandy-haired or dark blond man, sometimes this person has light-brown or gray hair. Light-colored or dark blue to green eyes, rarely hazel. This is a person of power and if he or she does not have money they spend it like they do. They are usually mature, hearty individuals.

Where the king falls, he is surrounded by the meaning of that particular square. On square **4, 5, 6, 13, 14, 16, 18, 19, 22, 23, 31, 34, or 35**: romance and love.

When the card falls on square **1, 3, 7, 8, 9, 10, 11, 12, 15, 17, 20, 24, 26, 32, or 36**: the king will be of great influence and nearly impossible to do without.

When the card falls on square **2, 21, 25, 27, 28, 29, 30, or 33**: some problems may occur. In these cases, you may question the loyalty of the king. The situation will play out whatever the meaning of the card.

Queen of Diamonds: A light-haired, light-eyed woman who is mature and has an air of authority around her. She also tends to be prosperous (similar to the king of diamonds).

When the queen of diamonds falls on square **14, 22, 23, 24, or 32**: the queen signifies someone who will marry. The cards surrounding the queen would show what kind of personality she has.

When the card falls on square **1, 5, 6, 7, 8, 10, 11, 13, 15, 17, 20, 21, 25, 27, 30, 33, 34, or 36**: the queen denotes a supportive person. Whatever the square represents, it is the circumstances that either a queen decides to help or not.

When the card falls on square **2, 3, 4, 9, 12, 16, 18, 19, 26, 28, 29, 31, or 35**: you must be respectful in approaching the queen of diamonds—especially on these squares.

Jack of Diamonds: A light-haired, light-eyed male or female; it is usually a young man. This person is great company and can have a very important but subtle impact on your life.

When the jack of diamonds falls on square **1, 3, 6, 7, 9, 12, 17, 18, 20, 21, 24, 26, 28, or 34:** this person will work closely with you to help you realize success; the meaning of the square will show how the jack will help.

When the card falls on square **2, 4, 5, 13, 14, 15, 16, 19, 22, 23, 25, 29, 31, 32, or 35:** the jack would either be a lover or a partner that had great influence over you.

When the card falls on square **8, 10, 11, 27, 30, 33, or 36:** a disappointment over a person who resembles the jack of diamonds would result. Again, the main concern is to remember the square's meaning.

King of Clubs: A dark-haired, dark-eyed man who is ambitious and driven; he always seems to know what to do. This person usually has a good sense of self. Remember, the meaning of the squares is as important as with any other face card.

When the king of clubs falls on square **1, 3, 6, 8, 11, 15, 17, 19, 20, 21, 24, 26, 27, 30, 32, or 35:** the king would be a key player for success.

When the card falls on square **2, 4, 9, 13, 14, 16, 18, 22, 23, 25, 29, or 31:** the king signifies a coworker or loved one.

When the card falls on square **5, 7, 10, 12, 28, 33, 34, or 36:** the king of clubs is someone who you need; this person does not necessarily need you.

Queen of Clubs: A dark-haired woman with dark eyes, surrounded by a little bit of mystery. This person usually has very definite ideas and is known to be stubborn.

When the queen of clubs falls on square **2, 5, 7, 8, 9, 12, 15, 19, 20, 21, 26, 29, 32, or 36**: these squares represent the meaning of a person who looks like the queen and how she would benefit you in numbers.

When the card falls on square **1, 3, 10, 17, 24, 25, 27, 28, 30, 33, or 34**: the help of the queen of clubs is invaluable.

When the card falls on square **4, 6, 11, 13, 14, 16, 18, 22, 23, 31, or 35**: the queen of clubs is a lover or partner.

Jack of Clubs: A brunette to dark-haired individual with dark eyes; this person is a strong individual with ideals and goals to match a particular dream.

When the jack of clubs falls on square **1, 4, 5, 6, 7, 11, 19, 20, 21, 26, 27, 29, 34, or 35**: these squares will manifest the jack with even stronger heights; keep in mind that the nature of the square is how it will come into being.

When the card falls on square **2, 8, 9, 10, 12, 17, 24, 28, 30, 33, or 36**: with such great ideas, you both make an unusual team; a very intense relationship with the jack of clubs.

When the card falls on square **3, 13, 14, 15, 16, 18, 22, 23, 25, 31, or 32**: a strong love affair that is overpowering at times.

King of Spades: A dark man in hair and eyes. A strong personality, this person is a survivor with a sense of humor and makes a wonderful leader.

When the king of spades falls on square **1, 3, 6, 9, 11, 17, 20, 21, 24, 26, 28, 30, 33, 35, or 36:** The relationship with the square reflects the relationship. In the case of the king of spades, this person will play a helpful role in a way that you least expect.

When the card falls on square **2, 4, 10, 12, 13, 14, 15, 16, 18, 22, 23, 25, 29, 31, or 32:** a strong love affair or marriage.

When the card falls on square **5, 7, 8, 19, 27, or 34:** working with the king of spades brings greatness against defeat.

Queen of Spades: A dark person in hair and eyes. This individual is in control, but frequently has the edge of tragedy around her.

When the queen of spades falls on square **1, 3, 7, 9, 12, 17, 18, 19, 26, 29, 32, 33, or 36:** a woman matching this description would be important to ensure success.

When the card falls on square **2, 13, 14, 15, 16, 22, 23, 24, 25, 31, or 34:** if you are interested in romance or love, these squares hold the key.

When the card falls on square **4, 5, 6, 8, 10, 11, 20, 21,27, 28, 30, or 35:** Team up with—not against—the queen of spades to ensure smooth sailing.

Jack of Spades: A young man or woman with dark eyes and hair; has a strong personality and intensity in whatever they do.

When the jack of spades falls on square **6, 9, 13, 14, 15, 16, 18, 21, 22, 23, 26, 29, or 31:** romance or a lover. Are you involved with a project that does not seem to be going anywhere?

When the card falls on square **1, 2, 3, 5, 11, 12, 19, 24, 27, 28, 32, or 35:** enlist the help of the jack of spades to get the job done.

When the card falls on square **4, 7, 8, 10, 17, 20, 25, 30, 33, 34 or 36:** not being able to agree can cause hardship or problems. Let the jack of spades help or get out of that person's way.

Sample Reading: Bill

This is a reading I gave to an artist and teacher who wanted to know how to find another position and what kind of work he should do. He asked a ton of questions.

Bill: What are you doing? Have you done this layout before?

Sophia: Yes, but it is really a difficult way to read the cards; a very complicated way called the Master spread or method. My grandmother and a very gifted psychic Gypsy friend of mine also did it, but they were very good. This spread is great for in-depth readings. It is an extremely old layout, and one not used much today. This system tends to be more black and white than most.

The Queen of Diamonds in the first house is a light-haired woman with money who is also powerful. This is an auspicious card; she will help you get a project through and would do a good job. She is probably an editor with light-colored eyes, probably gray.

Bill: Who is this?

Sophia: It is a woman who is in charge of a lot; she is probably an editor at a publishing house, someone who—you would be working directly with. Either that or someone in acquisitions. This is a major project, the first square is for the project in hand, for your work.

Bill: That makes sense.

Sophia: The second square is satisfaction. With the seven of spades you're not going to be happy with something the queen of diamonds will come up with. The third square has the three of hearts, so your project will be successful and you will also be successful. It will bring you money and all the good things like that. You have many aspirations for some projects. The fourth square with the jack of clubs is someone you hope to keep contact with. Jacks are go-getters and a jack of clubs would have dark hair and eyes. This is a person that you hope to have help you. The cards surrounding this one are strong, helpful cards. Some of the best cards you can get, really; they're what you want. They're what you truly hope can happen right now.

Bill: I saw a picture of a man who will probably be my agent. He fits this description very well.

Sophia: Chance or luck is very good right now. I am talking modest success, not millions, but thousands of dollars.

Bill: Well, the book I am thinking about still has to be written.

Sophia: You're talking about a project that is taking place now. With the four of hearts in the fifth square, this would indicate that you have a very good chance of having a successful project work.

Bill: This project is about a book I completed this week. I sent off the manuscript.

Sophia: You're right, it is about what you're doing now. The sixth square is the nine of hearts; it is an excellent card for wishes and desires. It means that almost everything you want, you're going to get.

Bill: That is nice.

Sophia: The ten of hearts would be better, but with the nine you're only one point away. It is an excellent card to have in this square. The injustice square is covered by the six of diamonds. If something happens unfavorably to you, the six of diamonds would help everything turn out in your favor. The past would finally be made right.

Bill: Good.

Sophia: Ingratitude, ten of diamonds, people who have not been respectful or have not had much gratitude toward you, because you have the ten of diamonds....

Bill: What are diamonds?

Sophia: Money, coins, earthly goods, and possessions; hearts are romance and love; spades are difficulties; and clubs are work. The next square is associations. The card covering it is the two of diamonds. Again, this is who you associate with; it is a very good card. It means you have favorable people in your life. The next square is loss; with the ace of diamonds this is very auspicious. This card would be somebody else's loss and you would be the one who gained. Either through someone's death or his or her surrendering of objects, you would turn out the winner.

Bill: Interesting.

Sophia: Okay. Number eleven is trouble—the jack of diamonds is in this square; again it is a person. Jacks sometimes can be women, but they are young, aggressive women. What is interesting is that it is near loss and this person who is next to the ace of diamonds is this. With a wild card as the ace, the loss will come to you, but ultimately will turn around and affect the jack of diamonds. This card would be a woman or a man who will try to make some trouble for you. The coloring of the jack is a brunette; it is interesting that the jack is a turn of faith that can help you.

Bill: It makes sense. A younger, nasty woman is making trouble for my book.

Sophia: The next square is a state or condition with the three of clubs; it means that the state you're in is not great. It seems that you have worked very hard. You don't look at things as small projects, molehills are a mountain for you right now, and that is your state and condition. You're very overwhelmed.

Bill: Okay. That is right on.

Sophia: Square thirteen is joy with the six of hearts; again, a lot of good things for you; a lot of joy and spontaneity. The next square is love and it has in it the six of spades. You feel that you don't get the love you deserve. You do feel supported or loved.

Bill: Hmm. Maybe so.

Sophia: The following square is prosperity with the nine of diamonds. You're going to have prosperity and money coming to you. What is interesting in this reading is that you have many projects and much money coming to you.

Bill: That is great.

Sophia: But your state or condition is not great. You're not that satisfied, and you don't feel that you get the love you need.

Bill: Sack of woe.

Sophia: Marriage in the sixteenth square has the two of hearts and that is very good; that means there is love in your marriage.

Bill (smiles): That is true.

Sophia: The next square is sorrow; things that should affect you adversely do not. You're doing well with many things. Because this square has the seven of diamonds, you have learned to shrug things off.

Pleasure and enjoyment are in the next square. With the nine of spades you're not having a good time; you don't go out and enjoy yourself. Whenever I see a card like this in a reading, I tell the person that they need to go out and have a good time. You need to do the things you want to do because you're not—it doesn't mean a thing if the other cards are good and you're not enjoying yourself. You're dissatisfied with your life and you don't like the condition of things, you feel unloved. Your cards say, "Hey, you have all these great projects and money coming to you, but you're unable to enjoy yourself."

Bill: I am in pain. I'm scheduled for oral surgery. I'm overworked and underpaid. Other than that, my life is great.

Sophia: In the inheritance or prosperity square, you have the ace of clubs—it's a wild card. It looks like you will get money or property that you were not expecting.

Bill: Really?

Sophia: Maybe your dad or mom will send you something that has been in your family; something you wanted. Or maybe you're mentioned in a will. With the ace of clubs, it is really a past card.

Bill: Interesting.

Sophia: The next square is fraud and deceit. In this square is the ten of hearts, which is a beautiful card. You will win over anyone who tries to get one over on you or who is deceitful. You're so blessed right now, and people are going to try to screw with you. Fraud and deceit is the nastiest place and you have one of the best cards. If anyone tries anything, you're not even going to feel it. You'll be totally unaware of it.

Bill: Good.

Sophia: The next square is rivals. You have the five of diamonds in this square, so you have no competition at the present time. Things are going well for you.

Bill: These cards are beautiful, they really are—especially seeing them laid out like this. They are striking. They are really nice, I love them; you never see cards like this. Oh, sorry—go on.

Sophia: The jack of hearts is in the next square, which is a present or gift. A blond-haired, blue-eyed person will give you a gift.

Bill: Oh, okay.

Sophia: This square is a lover; with the seven of hearts it shows you have a lover who is important to you. Even though you don't think you get the love you deserve, you really do.

Bill (laughs).

Sophia: Advancement is the next square, which is the eight of spades. You're not advancing as far as you want; it seems that hard and difficult obstacles have held you back—but you're headed for immediate change.

Bill: Interesting...true

Sophia: The next space is kindness or a good turn. With the seven of clubs, things have been pretty one- sided for you. It is others who should be giving and you really don't feel that. This is a case of getting the paper end of the lollipop.

Bill: True.

Sophia: Undertaking enterprise is the next square. With the five of clubs there, you do have your work ahead of you. Your nose will be at the grindstone to achieve what you want.

Bill: Makes sense.

Sophia: The next is the square of changes; in that square we have the queen of clubs. A woman of dark hair and dark eyes will affect you or change things around for you. She will bring changes into your life.

The king of clubs is next to her in the square of the end. This usually means the end of life and it would be somebody who will pass on. The death will greatly affect the queen of clubs; these are indications that somebody is not doing well.

Bill: Relatives of my wife are ill and very old.

Sophia: The next square is rewards, which is the four of clubs; it seems that you're not getting the rewards you want. It is interesting because the reality does not fit with what you want; things are better than what you feel. Square number thirty is misfortune or disgrace. With the four of diamonds, you have no misfortune, but you do have the ten of spades in the square of happiness. Happiness has been a long time coming; you have not been happy in a long time, have you?

Bill: I don't know. Sometimes, I guess; at work no way; with my writing, not so much.

Sophia: Family?

Bill: Oh, yeah, they're fine.

Sophia: Nine of clubs in the money or fortune square; it doesn't seem enough. Everything you own you've worked for. It is a good time to maybe start working for yourself.

Bill: That is true.

Sophia: Indifference space shows the four of spades. You can sometimes take things as they come, but normally it is hard for you to shrug things off. Life can bother you a bit.

Bill: Hmm.

Sophia: Next is the square of favors. Again, nobody is going to do much for you; with the three of spades there you're on your own. Nobody helps you. What is interesting is the ace of hearts in the ambition square; there is not really a better card to go here. What is interesting is your projects and ambitions, your goals in life, are doing great. But there are lots of disappointments with people in day-to-day life.

Bill: Day-to-day life sucks, this is true. My day-to-day life really is not good. My weekend is a perfect example. I baby-sat on Saturday and hung out. Today I went to the beach for an hour (laughs). So that was it for fun for all week. But projects, I think are going great or well.

Sophia: The king of spades is in the last square of, or sickness. This would probably be your father; you might want to get in contact with him.

Bill: Strange. I was going to call him this weekend. I have been wondering how he is doing.

Sophia: In conclusion, is there anything you want to ask?

Bill: What should I do to get a new job?

Sophia: Well, you have people who want to help you. The main thing for you is not to get discouraged. You have a lot of fortunate cards. It is best to remember that it may take you a while to find exactly what you want, but do not, whatever you do, get discouraged. You need to push forward; you have many heart and diamond cards that help and ease things along. You cannot be so sad. That goes against the energy of the cards, making it difficult to accomplish what you want. The cards in the lower part of the reading are more clubs and spades, causing difficulties. How this translates is that often you don't really want to look for another job, due to how much work it is to look for another job.

Bill: That's true.

Sophia: That's what the five of clubs in the undertaking enterprises square is all about. It is a card that finds it difficult to do much.

Bill: I'm discouraged. I'm not sure in what direction to go or what I want—except the writing and all these projects you said are favorable. Maybe that is what I should do; send out resumes, but not worry about them so much. Just go to work and write the next book. Not to think that much about getting a new job right now.

Sophia: Apply for only the jobs you really want and don't worry about the timing. I would spend the month of February taking the time to put together and send out your resume and any book proposals.

Bill: Oh, yes, I plan on doing that the next week or two.

Sophia: Well, that will take care of the month of February for you.

Bill: You were also talking about all the people you see in this reading; are they actually people?

Sophia: Yes, the queen of clubs is probably your wife because that is what she looks like. Changes!

Bill: She is going through menopause (both laugh). Just kidding....

Sophia: The clubs are people who are nearing the end of life.

Bill: I know who they are.

Sophia: This is someone who is ill.

Bill: That is probably my dad. Thank you very much; that was very interesting, I really enjoyed it. I imagine it is like the tarot, that the cards around it mean something.

Sophia: Yes, that is right.

Bill: Very interesting patterns around some of the cards, a very interesting system, a lot of cards are used. It is odd that every spot is discussed.

Sophia: This is a very old system and it is difficult to master.

Bill: It is incredibly accurate and the system is based on six. Any system based on six is extremely old and comes from the Sumerians. Their whole systems are based on six.

Sophia: The only people whom I have seen use this system were extremely adept at cards and excellent readers. This is such an old system. It was twenty years ago that I first saw it being used by my grandmother and my friend, Mrs. Ryser. They were close to their seventies and learned how to read when they were young. The cards are an oral tradition, so who knows how long this one cartomancy layout has been going on. Many times, I have seen only a portion of the cards turned over. If you don't want to know everything, why would you?

Bill: How interesting. So let's say if a person only wanted to know about misfortune, he or she would only turn over a few cards, then throw the rest away.

Sophia: Right.

Bill: That is so cool. What an interesting idea; you lay them all out. If all you're interested in is some money issues, that is what cards you would turn over.

Sophia: Exactly. If someone came to our home for a reading and we did not particularity care for that person, we wouldn't waste much time with them. My grandmother wouldn't turn over every card. At that time, readings were different. If you came for a reading, you could never question the psychic's ability. You would never ask the psychic why they didn't turn over every card. You would never question a psychic; you did a trade or would bring a gift. If you wanted a good reading, you would approach it from a level of respect and not demand any more than what the reader was willing to give. If the reader liked you, he or she was helpful. If not, the reader wouldn't give you much time. Those readers didn't suffer fools gladly, as my grandmother would say.

Bill: Well, back then psychics had power and people were more respectful.

Sophia: Any psychic who takes money should be well versed in these matters. Really, that is why people question their readers now. They are paying for a service; it is their right to question. It is the nineties. Psychics in the past accepted donations. I have broken with the tradition by taking money for reading services, but this has made readings very different for me; I always continue for an hour. In my grandmother's house that was rare.

Bill: Money changes everything.

Sophia: Do you have any other question? Your hour is almost up (both laugh).

Bill: Thank you. I feel so much better and I have more insight into my life. Much more than an hour ago.

Sample Reading: Robert

This is a reading from the Master spread for a client who owns Mandala Books, a bookstore, and who has been involved with the occult for some time. He had never had his playing cards read and was looking forward to a different kind of divination.

Sophia: This is the Master card reading. It is a difficult spread, but is the most thorough one I have ever seen. After I have shuffled the cards and put them into three piles, please put the cards in one pile.

Robert: This is a nice looking deck, too.

Sophia: What is great about this spread is that I don't have to go into great detail with someone. If they have only a couple of questions and don't want to know about their whole life, I can turn over the cards that they have questions about. I am going to read all your cards, though.

Robert: Well, I can understand that. Many people have the same issues over and over again. Does everyone use a full deck?

Sophia: Some people remove some of the cards when they are going to do a reading, like all the twos and threes, something like that. I don't do that. I feel that every card has a special significance; otherwise it would not be in the deck in the first place.

The first card is a project in hand, which is the ace of clubs. What this means is that you have major projects that are a lot of work. Major goals, high aspirations, and a lot of work are ahead of you. With the ace of clubs, I have to tell you, you cannot control the energy. Clubs are work, so this ace is wild work; your work is erratic. Real highs or real lows. The energy will be fine if you don't try to control it and let the chips fall where they may. If you try to control it, it is harder.

The next square is satisfaction with the queen of diamonds in it. She has light brown hair and light eyes. This personality is generous and nice and generally has money. She has no problem with helping other people; she is a giving person.

Next is the queen of clubs in the square of success. Now the queen of clubs is a dark woman and the coloring of the queen of clubs is like me. Dark hair and dark eyes. This person is usually work- and goal-oriented. She is a worker and has things she wants to do. She is a busy person and is the business woman of the deck.

In the fourth square is the ten of hearts; this square represents hope. You have much hope and many desires; the ten of hearts shows that—you will realize this soon. You cannot get a better card than that. This card is very strong, so your hopes and desires will really be there all the time.

Following, in the fifth square, is chance and luck with the three of diamonds. This means you have a wonderful opportunity in whatever you want to do next.

The next card is wishes and desires with the ten of clubs. You find it difficult to get what you want; but with such a high number you're close to achieving some long-term options and desires. So, realizing your projects and your hopes is huge expectations, very high ideals.

The first line of cards is the line of hope and wishes. You can get a sense of what is going on in your life and where you want to be by looking at this first line. Looking at the ten of clubs; it is a very high number. Then over here you have the ace of clubs, which is in the project-at-hand space. You definitely do what you love even though you question what you're doing. Then you have the two queen cards and they fit the physical description of your roommates and business partners. With the heart and diamond cards, there is a great chance for having your dreams realized

Robert: Tell me more about the queens.

Sophia: They have the coloring and looks of your partners, and the personality types as well. If all of you want to go in a different direction and try out some new ideas, you will be successful.

Let's go to the next line of cards. Injustice with the ten of spades—be careful of signing anything right now. Read the fine print on any deals or contracts that come across your desk. The injustices are wrongdoings to you from somebody else.

The next space is the two of clubs in the ingratitude square. You frequently feel that you're being taken advantage of, but only in little things. With the two queen cards you feel that they have a certain advantage over you. Not a lot, but a little of it can build resentment. The great thing about the cards is that you can change your reality, you can do card spells. Then you can switch things around to how you'd like. The five of diamonds follows in the association square. The queen of clubs has great connections, people in high places?

Robert: Yes, that is true. She used to be in show business.

Sophia: It looks like the associations she has will run off on you. Also, you're being invited to parties; your social life is picking up. Next is losses; four of clubs means minor losses. Four is not a real high number, but you're experiencing some setbacks now. Things are stirred up a bit, but I bet you like that.

Robert: Yes, I do a bit.

Sophia: In the tenth space is the three of clubs; a little trouble at work.

The next is the space for state or condition; the six of spades is here. With this card, I have to be honest, you will have some obstacles here in conflict with your desires and needs, but it will work out. You want this because if it was too easy it would not feel like it was yours.

The next is joy with the six of clubs; it is kind of hard to enjoy yourself. It is difficult for you to relax and enjoy yourself. It is hard for you to go out and relate to others. This is a card that can get you stuck, so watch it. Next is the ace of hearts in the card space of love. This is just about the best card for love. I believe that you will be meeting someone nice.

Robert: That would be nice, I'm about due.

Sophia: You cannot do better than the love card in the love circle. Next is the prosperity space with the ace of diamonds. You're going to have big money coming in this year.

Robert: I have had a pretty good feeling about this year in general.

Sophia: This is really big money; this is really nice. Next in the marriage circle is the king of diamonds. I have seen the king of diamonds representing some women, but they are powerful women—a person who can hold her own. Do you like strong women? This is the kind of partner you're comfortable with, someone who can hold her own. She has light hair, but not a blond. She has a kick-ass personality, so I hope you're into goddess worship. She will demand that you worship the ground she walks on.

The king of hearts in the place of sorrow or affliction; this card looks like your good buddy Bill. It is the person you go to in crises. Either the both of you or one of you will go to the other for consolation.

Next is the seven of diamonds in the place of pleasure or enjoyment. When you do something you want to do, you can enjoy yourself. You probably love your alone time.

The next is another seven, the seven of hearts in inheritance or prosperity. Money coming from your family; looks good, you don't have to worry.

The fraud and deceit space has the five of spades; this is a warning card. Again, be careful; check out any contracts that you sign. This is not the time to seal a deal with a handshake.

With the ten of spades in the injustice square, you're given a message to watch your butt. Five of hearts is in the place of rivals—even your competition doesn't cause that much problem for you.

Next is the present space with the five of clubs. Lots of fives—you have the five of hearts, spades, and now clubs. You're into the Kabala so you can see the deeper significance of the cards, lots of Mars energy. With the five of clubs, any present that you receive will have some sort of duty tied into it.

The next space is the lovers with the seven of spades. You're a bit cautious in a relationship. You want one but sometimes you hold back and sometimes you think the king of diamonds is the person for you. Then sometimes you think the queen of spades is the perfect one for you but we have not reached that one yet.

Advancement, rising in the world, shows the six of hearts. This is how you want to see yourself. You want love and respect and there is no reason why you cannot have that.

The next card is the jack of spades in the place of a kindness or a good turn. This is a dark younger man, probably your friend Scott or someone like that who is going to do something nice for you for no reason—just because he is a nice guy. Sometimes the jack of spades is a young woman, but they are very brassy.

Jack of diamonds is here in the undertaking enterprises square. This is also someone who would help you along. Again, it is the dishwater blond or light brown hair type. I bet these two are friends and help each other along and have wonderful ideas. It looks like you're going to be approached by two people who want to use your space for other stuff you didn't even think about. Some of those ideas are going to be really good. You have to very careful of the money and of contracts. Make sure there are no misunderstandings, although you can tell your friends down here what is going on. It is good to be completely honest and not give a lot away at this time.

Next is the nine of hearts in the changes square. Everything is going to change for the better, really in a big way.

The queen of spades is next, in the end of life square. Basically, this square means the end or death. This is a dark woman, but the person doesn't always have to have dark hair and dark eyes; they can be dark in personality. Whoever she is, she is over or gone; she represents an ending.

Robert: We know who that is.

Sophia: The cards surrounding the queen show that life has worked out for the better. Good riddance. Reward square is next with the two of diamonds. That is a good card; you feel you're going to be rewarded for your past work in a not so big way.

Next is the square of misfortune and disgrace. Misfortune cards for you are all fours; a four of spades and four of clubs in the loss square. You can also look at this as a measure of time—four days, four weeks, or four months. It is probably four weeks; with the cards, everything speeds up. After a reading you will see that things start to speed up. The cards are great catalysts.

Robert: They are very mercurial.

Sophia: I believe that is why they turned into gambling tools and why they are popular in folk magick spells. Their very nature promotes change. Next is the eight of hearts in the square of happiness. Great happiness is coming your way.

Following is the eight of diamonds in the money and fortune square; again, luck is headed your way. Wow, Robert, this looks like it is going to be your year.

Nine of clubs is in indifference. You play down your success and you're really very modest about all your accomplishments.

The queen of hearts is going to ask you for a favor.

Robert: I know who that is (laughs).

Sophia: Next is the nine of diamonds in the ambition square. You have an amazing amount of ambition for this year; you're aiming high.

The king of clubs is in the last square; the square of sickness or ill health. Someone else is getting sick. Tell your dad to take care of himself. When you see a card like this it is often a parent or something.

Phew! That's a lot! Do you have any questions about this?

Robert: No, it all sounds pretty right on. Hope the good stuff happens!

Sophia: You should get a good idea what is going on, I hope.

Robert: I'm checking out the balance here. All four queens, all four fives, three aces, three sevens, three kings. This was really fun and an excellent reading. Thank you so much.

Chapter 9

Card Spells

You can use card spells to change the outcome of a situation or achieve the results you want—especially if you want to tip the scale in your own behalf one way or the other. If you want to alter what you had in a reading—perhaps change a card or two that indicates problems in the future—a card spell is a good way to do it. With little preparation, you can do card spells. All you need is a strong will, the cards, and a few items that are easy to find.

Most of my spells, including the ones you will find in this chapter, work with the twelve-house astrology system. I often use an image of the "wheel of the twelve houses" when doing spells. For example, when I was a teenager and wanted a date, I put a few jacks into the fifth house. I picked Wednesday night to start my spell (being a Gemini, Wednesday coincided with my sun sign, which is Mercury; Wednesday is also a good night for communication. Since I use an astrological spread, I believe it is best to pick one night that vibrates with your sign). When I did the spell, I always picked the fifth house because I wanted to have fun but did not want to be in a serious relationship. Sometimes, I threw in an ace to spice up the situation and a five of hearts to keep it running smoothly. After completing this spell, I always had plenty of dates by Friday night. My girlfriends also loved this spell because we always had dates and many parties to go to. My grandparents thought it was great that I was so popular and did not mind me using the card spells—as long as I did not use my spells to harm others.

The spells found in this chapter are not found in any other book because they were part of my family's oral tradition. I never saw these spells written down anywhere. To successfully complete them, you need to know about the Zodiac, but what you have picked up in this book already is certainly enough. If you feel unsure, reread chapter 4, "The Wheel of Life Spread." Creating a card spell is a simple process, but it is also wise to realize that just because you are asking something to manifest itself does not mean that it will happen exactly the way you want. At first, go easy and do not overdo it.

One of the best cards you can use in a card spell is an ace—especially a special ace in the first house, such as the ace of diamonds for going on a job interview. The interviewer will definitely remember you. It is best to start out performing simple card spells and not to cast influence over others directly.

Sometimes, I get the request to cast a spell over someone, especially to make one person love another. Why bother? It is easier to put your energy into yourself than try to influence another.

It is not wise, but you can use the cards with candles to bring a certain type of person to you, such as putting the king of hearts with the ten of diamonds over it in the seventh house. If you look up the meanings of these cards in chapter 5, the intent of this spell will become clear. See what I mean? The possibilities are endless.

Before you begin trying a card spell, you need to pick a day of the week that works with your sun sign, and a colored candle to set the mood.

First, pick a day of the week that works with your sun sign.

Monday:	The Moon	Cancer
Tuesday:	Mars	Aries, Scorpio
Wednesday:	Mercury	Gemini, Virgo
Thursday:	Jupiter	Sagittarius, Pisces
Friday:	Venus	Taurus, Libra
Saturday:	Saturn	Capricorn, Aquarius
Sunday:	Sun	Leo

You should also use your special day for reading for yourself. It is better to read the cards once or twice a week to gain experience. When I started, I read the cards every day to see the trends in my life and to become a good reader. Reading every day for yourself is not necessary, though, unless you want to be on top of things all the time or you want to read cards professionally.

Next, you need to pick a candle to set the mood and add to the magick. Candle colors are key to many spells; pick out the correct color to correspond with your desire. Pick out only one color, however, and do not use a blend.

If I want to have a truly effective candle, I will make my own. If you grew up in the seventies, you might remember that every town had a candle making shop. Today, however, you can buy the wax and other supplies at a hobby store. But you do not have to take candle making so seriously if you do not want to. It is all right to buy candles.

Following is a list of colors and what they can help you accomplish.

Red: Love, sex, passion

Black: Letting go, losing weight, binding, repelling, destroying

Green: Money, wealth, possessions

Blue: Health, healing, relaxing your mind and spirit

White:	Inspiration, wisdom, insight
Purple:	Fun, entertainment, parties
Orange:	Travel, learning, education
Yellow:	Attraction, promotion, goals
Pink:	Romance, beauty, children

Now that you have selected a day and chosen a candle, you are almost ready to start. If you want a long-term spell to work, you must do the spell for a longer period of time. For example, if you want a new and better job— maybe one you have wanted for a long time— the card spell will take longer. For the best results, start the spell on the full moon and end on the full moon, after a complete lunar cycle. The trick is that you must light the candle and meditate on what you want at the same time every day. You need to focus on what kind of job you want and how you will get it. It is also important to be realistic. You do not want to say you want to be a brain surgeon with a high school education. Think about your interests and what you can really do— these are the key things.

It is best not to be vague with what you want. To say you want a good job and make a lot of money will help—but you will probably end up in a different type of work than what you had in mind. The cards, although really strong, will not change your life unless you put energy into your own life. Sometimes you need to move forward. The cards will help you, but only if you make an effort yourself.

Once you start working a card spell, you must finish it; and you must also be directed and focused. Do not spend your time changing what you asked for in the middle of a spell. Keep your meditation simple and direct. This formula works well and you can achieve results with a little planning and direction. The possibilities are endless.

Following are directions on how to do a spell if you want short-term gains and just want to play around. Still, even if you feel it is a game, think carefully about what you want— you might get it!

How to Make a Spell

On a large sheet of paper, draw the twelve houses as a big twelve-sectioned wheel. Make the wheel large enough so that a card can fit into each section. You can even use the appropriate color pen, depending on the mood you want to set.

Once you have put the cards in the circle (choose one from the "Card Combinations" section below), you will draw a circle around each card to make it look protected. Remember, this is your desire, so do not let any cards outside of the protected circle; they need to stay in their house. Do not remove the cards until you are finished with the spell, and do not allow others to touch them. This is your spell and no one else's.

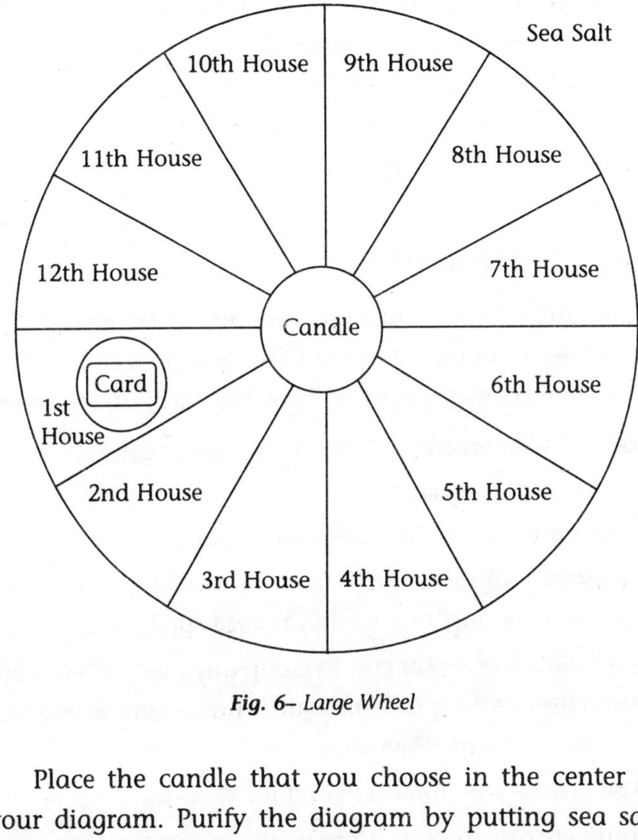

Fig. 6– Large Wheel

Place the candle that you choose in the center of your diagram. Purify the diagram by putting sea salt around the outside of it. On the chosen day, at a time when you will not be disturbed, center yourself and meditate on the cards that you want and your desires coming true. You probably already have a good idea of what you want or you would not be going this far to obtain your dreams. A powerful intent and desire need to be present to have spells work. Once you have a clear idea what you want, pick your cards carefully.

When the spell is finished, end it by saying something appropriate. Dispose of the salt in a natural way (for example, you can put it in a stream or bury it). Do not forget to mentally and psychically see all the energy take off when you dispose of the salt.

Card Combinations

Some cards make great combinations, others do not. You can chose from one of my old family recipes or make up your own. Following are some possible card combinations.

4 aces: a wild time in any house and out of control energy.

4 kings: very different men (great for vacations); best to pick only one for the lunar card spell.

4 queens: four different women (or men if you are gay); best to pick only one for lunar card spell.

4 jacks: a lot of fun or can liven up any place; do not put this combination in your fourth house unless you like living in cramped quarters.

4 ten cards: very intense; good for results.

4 nine cards: strong but not as intense as the tens.

4 eight cards: only for major changes in combination with other cards.

4 seven cards: good luck.

4 six cards: starting to achieve results.

4 five cards: success but not as strong as the tens.

4 four cards: not great for spells, avoid them; minor inconveniences; good for messing with someone else's life.

4 three cards: in any combination, too minor to use.

4 two cards: small beginnings; not the best for spells in any combination.

You can also use the above in combinations of threes and twos of a kind or number, but the results are much more minor. If you use only one card, the spell will be much more directed. To create your own unique combination, look up what card you want in chapter 2, "The Meanings of the Cards," and pick your own guide. Do not forget to see what that card means in chapter 5, "Card Meanings for the Wheel of Life Spread." Some cards are not so great in certain houses. The sky's the limit, however, and there are some fun combinations. Here are some tried-and-true combinations.

The ace of hearts and diamonds: in any of the houses for a change in your life.

Choose any face card: either pick a card that is you or the person you want to bring or influence, put it in the house you desire, and put a ten of hearts to cover it. See what happens. Love will come to you if put it in the first or seventh house. Interested in a coworker? Try the tenth house.

The five of hearts: for fun in the fifth house.

The ten of diamonds in the tenth house: for a promotion at work.

The spades: are not the best to use for yourself if you want to gain something, but try putting them in someone else's house (such as the eighth) if you want distance or to repel another.

A Card Spell Example

I put the two of spades in the eighth house along with the jack of clubs to relieve me of an individual who was bothering me. Even though I told him it was over, he still pursued and followed me (they call it stalking today). I had no life and no one else would date me because he threatened all who came near me—even my female friends received nasty notes on their car windshields. This man came from a well-respected family and was wealthy; the authorities told me it was my problem. I asked the council of my family and they suggested sending him away with the cards. My family knew he did not mean any harm, but he did not see any options in his life. When I visualized him leaving, I placed him in another state, starting a new life and having a woman who would fit his needs. I also asked that he be driven out of my life and that I would have a new start in life with someone who would not be afraid to date me.

I picked a card that looked like the man who was bothering me, then I picked a card that would help get him from my life; the two of spades would make him annoyed at me, which would turn his attention to others. I added the ten of spades to ensure success. Then I put the ten of clubs in the ninth house to send him on his way so he would go out and find a long-term goal.

I knew that would send him on a journey. I took the jack and the ten of spades from the eighth house and touched the ninth house ten of clubs. This would propel him to his new life. I put the queen of clubs (my card) with a ten of hearts over me for protection in the first house. Then, to find a lover who had courage and was fun, I put a special card in the fifth house—the king of hearts. I put the ten of diamonds over it to protect him. The candle I chose was white for purity, wisdom, and an honest outcome.

My spell worked. The man went off to school in Boston and met a nice woman he could share his interests with. Although the jack never apologized, he left me in peace. I found someone who had similar interests as mine and we both worked at the same job.

It is best to give others positive options with spells like the one above. Sure, I could have cursed him and I was almost ready to; I was afraid and mad. My grandfather, however, told me that it is wrong to hurt when you have the power to heal. My spell liberated both of us and the man was none the wiser about what helped him along. It does not matter that it might not have happened if I did not do the spell. What matters is that it happened because of some cosmic push by the cards.

The main thing is to think carefully, plan well, experiment, and see what happens. Try small spells weekly first, then see how it goes from there.

Other Card Spell Spreads

Other card spreads exist that are also worth mentioning for spells. These other spreads do not have an astrological slant, but the meaning of everything else is the same. With a little creative thought, you can use any layout for spells.

There is the four-card spread, which is great for a quick reading or simple magick and also beneficial for learning how to do both. This is how I learned to read the cards and it is a wonderful way to develop psychic powers. The cards are laid out as mentioned in chapter 3, "The Small Star Spread." The spell follows the ideas of the reading, but in an active manner; you are making it happen, not reading what will happen.

There is also nothing to stop you from drawing a simple circle and using one, two, or a few cards for simple spells. Make sure you use the salt and a candle as mentioned above.

The aces are the most powerful cards to use. Following is an example of the most used ace, but keep in mind that any of them pack the same kick.

If you use the ace of hearts in a card spell, you can win over anybody. This ace is a dynamic card that, if used wisely, can greatly benefit you. One word of caution, only use this card with someone you truly love; it is unfair to attract someone only to neglect that person later. When I was a teenager, I once used this card for a friend who asked me to help her get a certain guy. We both thought she loved him because all she ever talked about was how cute this guy was. He never paid any attention to her and, really, I do not think he knew she existed. I said that I would help her so I did the spell with the ace of hearts and a red candle—and the next time he saw her it was love at first sight.

He started to call her every day and told her he did not know what was wrong with him— he said he had never felt this way before and that he loved her. My friend, however, was no longer interested; she was only interested in him for the love of the chase. He was hurt that she did not reciprocate his love and I felt like a jerk. I swore that I would never do another spell for a person—and I haven't broken that vow yet. Even if you are sure you love someone who does not love you, just wait. The ace of hearts is that powerful. This should give you an idea about the true power of the cards!

APPENDIX

Cartomancers I Have Known

The Hougan

My husband, our small son, and I took a trip to New Orleans and stayed with an old friend of my husband's. His friend is a priest in the Voudon Spiritual Temple and asked us if we wanted to come to a practice drumming service. We went along to watch him drum and meet his friends.

The temple was amazing with its various altars. When the music started, the whole room changed. Because I am a ritualist photographer, the Hougan (High Priest) Oswan asked me to photograph various altars and told me not to forget anything. My husband presented the Hougan with a book he had written (Global Ritualism). The Hougan loved it. He looked it over and talked with my husband. They discussed initiation, his life in Belize, and how he found his way to the United states. The Priestess arrived, beautiful and self-confident in her power; her energy overtook an entire room. She brought down a Loa (god) and danced. Then she purified us all with cigar smoke as the god Ogun possessed her. The power was amazing.

Later, my husband mentioned to the Hougan that I knew how to read playing cards. The Hougan asked to see me in his kitchen because he too read cards. We discussed the variation of how we both read playing cards, the similarities, and where we learned. He was taught in Belize, also by oral tradition. We discussed differences with the way we read the cards. It is interesting to note how, for us, the cards pretty much meant the same things. In his system, though, he used every card in a reading. Both of us also used astrology in our card readings. In my system, the place where the card lands is a house and is then given astrological signifiers. With him, it is the card that denotes astrological significance. For example, the king of diamonds would be an Aquarius. Also in his system, different suits have connections with animals, terrain, and many other symbols. We both agreed that playing cards were more interesting to us than tarot cards.

When I asked him why he was so interested in them, he told me he found them so mysterious. He also told me how he was initiated into Voudon, and the ceremonies that he took to become a Hougan. I asked him why he was telling me all the secrets he knew about the cards. He said that I knew the value of the cards and that "I should stir it up." He started to wave his hands into the air as if smoke from a cauldron was rising and disappearing. "Stir it up," he said, his hands rising higher and higher, "stir it up." After that he told me an intense transmission on cartomancy.

We left. The drumming had stopped and everything calmed down. Everyone in the temple started to come out drinking beer and move around the courtyard. We left to go eat dinner and got into the spirit of New Orleans—we partied at our friend's house until the wee hours in the morning. Then we received a telephone call from the high priestess, telling us that the Hougan was in the hospital. He died a few hours after the telephone call.

I was the last person who talked to him in depth. I was also the only person to whom he had discussed the playing cards and his system. It was an honor to meet him and his lovely wife. I am grateful that he found me worthy enough to pass down his information. I hope his cartomancy system sees print someday.

A Gypsy Woman

An old Gypsy woman who was very gifted as a psychic and card reader used to read my cards. Like my grandmother, she also used the Master spread. She taught me what to expect from a good reading. The first time I saw her, I had a total earthshaking experience because she was able to go into great details about my life, both in my past and in the present. The future was the most shocking part, though. She gave me details about what my future husband would look like and how we would meet. So far all that she told me has unfolded. This first reading was twenty years ago and it never ceases to amaze me how accurate she was. After meeting and talking with her, I decided to really go for it and develop my ability to be as good as she is.

A Chippewa Indian

A different cartomancer I met, very different, was a Chippewa Indian. I used to spend a lot of time with him and his family. We would drink coffee and eat Indian fry bread together. Most of our entertainment revolved around reading each other's playing cards. We both used the Wheel of Life spread and interpreted the cards the same way. He was originally from the Dakotas and learned on the reservation. Another oral tradition.

A final note

I have encountered only a few cartomancers in my life and each has been special and unique. I hope their card-reading traditions survive as this one will, now that it is in your hands. Good Fortune.